66947

ɔy-step decoupage.

DATE DUE			
FEB 20 19/9			

STEP-BY-STEP

DECOUPAGE

by Dee Davis and Dee Frenkel

Golden Press • New York

Western Publishing Company, Inc.
Racine, Wisconsin

A classic French print was used to enhance this graceful box. Parts of the
print were cut out and rearranged for
a repeated rhythm all around the sides;
two identical prints were used for the
details on the top. The background is
terra-cotta paint over polished gesso.
The finished box, with a marbled paper
lining and elegant brass feet, is illustrated on page 33.

Acknowledgments

We would like to thank the following artists whose work appears in this book:
John F. Campbell, Carl Federer, Nellie Goldmark, Sally Anne Kellogg, Alberta and
John Lloyd-Evans, Edith Loening, Ruth Newkirk, Marian Rubinstein, Ann Voorhees,
Lenore M. Crowley, Ernie Furtado, Judy Johnson, Ruth Lipston, Mildred Misura,
Barbara Roth, Ruth Steckman, and Francisco Solis. We would also like to thank:
Lew Davis, Dottie Jessup, Susan Giddins, Judy and Doug Johnson, Nancy Siegel,
Alice Straus, and Lee Walker; and to extend our appreciation to the Bernard Pic-
ture Co., Inc., Connoisseur Studio, Inc., and the Donald Art Co., Inc.

Dee Davis and Dee Frenkel

Art Director: Remo Cosentino
Art Assistant/Diagrams: Diane Wagner
Editor: Caroline Greenberg
Photographs: George Ancona

Library of Congress Catalog Card Number: 75-10926

Contents

Introduction

Decoupage (pronounced day-coo-pahj) is the art of decorating surfaces with applied paper cutouts. The process of transforming a simple object into an objet d'art requires the mastering of a few basic techniques; once mastered, they become the means to an infinitely satisfying creative experience, with results that are not only useful, but original and beautiful as well. The possibilities of decoupage are almost limitless, and the various steps you will take in creating a beautiful object that reflects your own individuality and taste are truly exciting ones.

The French derivation of the word decoupage is from *découper*—to cut out. Hiram Manning, a leading authority on eighteenth-century decoupage, describes it as the art of the four Cs: coloring, cutting, composing, and covering. It is "the art of decorating surfaces with paper that has been colored, cut, assembled, and glued according to one's own design." In *The Limitless World of Decoupage,* Dorothy Harrower explains that decoupage is made from "cut-outs that are redesigned to depict a scene, to re-create a period, to tell a story, or to decorate a plain surface."

During the flowering of decoupage in eighteenth-century Italy, apprentices decorated furniture with hand-colored engravings to imitate the expensive, hand-painted furniture that was then in vogue. Though the master painters of the time whose work was being imitated disparaged decoupage as *l'arte del povero* (the poor man's art), many beautiful pieces of furniture were produced. The secretaries, chests of drawers, and tables ornately embellished with hand-colored engravings that can occasionally be seen in museums today are a testament to the fine craftsmanship of these early decoupeurs.

The mid-eighteenth century also saw the emergence of a vogue for chinoiserie and lacquer work in Europe, and the decoupage of this period reflects it. Oriental prints were cut out and pasted onto painted furniture, and the entire surface was then varnished. According to Hugh Honour, in his book *Chinoiserie,* the Remondini of Bassano, Italy, published a series of engravings in 1765 to be used for this purpose. In France, decoupage was a favorite pastime at the fashionable court of Marie Antoinette, where ladies cut up the engravings of Watteau, Boucher, Fragonard, and Pillement to decorate boxes, fans, and screens.

By the late eighteenth century, the art of decoupage had become a popular craft in England. The *Ladies' Amusement Book,* published in 1762, was a widely-used source for black and white prints to color and cut. The Victorian women who took up decoupage as a pastime used, among other things, gold paper braid and embossed scrapbook pictures from Germany, and prints from *Godey's Lady's Book* (1830–1898) for their decoupage.

For centuries, decoupage has been an important source of decoration in many countries. It is a craft to share, as people did in the past

This eighteenth-century Venetian secretary, painted in colors and gold, displays intricate applied engravings and a lacquer finish. (The Metropolitan Museum of Art, Fletcher Fund, 1925.)

when families and friends worked together and learned from each other. The revival of interest in decoupage is spreading rapidly now, to children as well as adults, and to men as well as women. Though many choose to work in the traditional styles, others are using modern styles and methods to create their own personal statements in decoupage.

As you continue working in decoupage and become more knowledgeable, your tastes may change; you may grow to prefer the classic eighteenth-century hand-colored style of decoupage, or you may come to prefer a more contemporary experimental style.

"Painting with scissors" is unique to decoupage; you can cut apart and combine several different prints to form an original, unusual design on all the surfaces of a three-dimensional object. Once you start, you will find yourself with more ideas than you can possibly execute, and you will begin to notice details, designs, and colors that will serve as constant sources of inspiration to you. As you look at objects with an eye to decorating them, and search for prints and paper to use, you will find yourself learning about design, composition, and color, and you will develop a "critical eye."

Lest you grow too critical of your efforts to achieve perfection, however, remember that being "perfect" and being exceptionally well-made are two different things entirely. The real beauty of a hand-crafted object is that it is *not* perfect—human hands, rather than machines, have formed it. As the great art historian John Ruskin said, "All things are literally better, lovelier and more beloved for the imperfections that reflect the *human* effort that went into their making."

"American Fantasy" (c. 1860). Cut paper with embossed details and water color on a blue ground. 15″ × 18″. Lebanon, Pennsylvania. (The Virginia Museum, Collection of Fred Wichmann.)

Materials and Equipment

SELECTING YOUR PROJECT

The object you choose to decoupage may be a "found object" such as a rock, a piece of bark, or a piece of driftwood, or it may be a functional object, made of almost anything from wood to metal. Raw wood is perhaps the best kind of surface for a beginner to decoupage, and the choice here is enormous. Most craft shops carry a selection of raw wood objects made of basswood or white pine, both of which are excellent for decoupage since they are fairly hard, close-grained woods. (Harder woods such as walnut, cherry, and maple are good to work on as well. Open-grained woods such as redwood should be avoided.)

If you have a local craft shop that carries decoupage supplies, you will probably find everything you need there. If you can't find what you want at your local craft shop, browse through antique and second-hand shops, and take another look at the "junk" you've consigned to your basement or attic—you may find the perfect thing to decoupage there. Most old wood and metal objects can be repaired, and, with a few additional steps, prepared for decoupage. Another excellent source of objects is the mail order decoupage supply house (see the list of suppliers on page 64).

One word of advice: Stick to simple, flat-surfaced items such as trays, plaques, or boxes for your first attempts. As you develop your skills as a craftsperson, you will learn how to handle more complicated and challenging projects such as lamps, complicated shapes, and pieces of furniture.

Prints. The selection of your print or reproduction will be a reflection of your taste and personality. There is an enormous range of pictures to choose from, so don't just settle for any picture—keep looking until you find something that really appeals to you.

In addition to craft shops that sell prints specially made for decoupage, museums, art supply stores, stationery stores, books, and magazines are excellent sources of pictures. Many bookstores sell engravings and prints, and art supply stores often carry prints of flowers and birds. Children's books, books about wildlife, and books about botany are very good sources for pictures as well. Old hand-colored prints and engravings are often extremely beautiful, but since they are usually fairly costly, save them for a time when you are more expert at decoupage.

Pay attention to the type of paper your print is on. The texture should be smooth, not grainy. The paper should be fairly thin, but paper that is *too* thin may wrinkle, or fail to hide glue. Heavy paper, such as postcard paper, and the paper from which some greeting cards are made, may have to be thinned (see page 18). Avoid coated glossy stock.

When selecting a print, bear in mind the size and shape of your object. Choose a print that has the right proportions for the object

A few examples of the great variety of raw wood objects suitable for decoupage. The larger boxes can be used for purses with the addition of handles, clasps, and hinges like those shown here.

you'll be working on. Avoid prints that will be very difficult to cut; simple, well-defined shapes that aren't too small are best. Fine, detailed cutting takes practice. If you use more than one print, make sure the elements are in proportion, and that they suit each other in color and style as well as the size and shape of your object.

There are many reproductions of old black and white engravings that are made for hand coloring. But since hand coloring takes a certain amount of practice, reserve it for future projects.

Background colors. Use a background appropriate to the subject and colors of the print you have chosen. Choosing a paint or stain in a lighter or darker shade of one of the print's major colors usually works very well. A soft pastel shade of one of the colors in the print will almost always provide an excellent background for it. Off-white paint looks like old ivory after it's been covered with many coats of varnish, and is a good neutral background for almost any color print.

Study the color wheel on page 60. The primary colors are red, yellow, and blue, and all other colors are made from them. Complementary colors are opposite each other on the wheel. These are orange and blue, red and green, yellow and purple. Colors that are adjacent to each other on the color wheel (for instance, purple, blue, and green, or red, orange, and yellow) are harmonious. (For other tips on color, see the section on Hand Coloring.)

Wood stains and glazes are transparent, so that the grain of the wood is visible under them. Metallic waxes of different colors enhance the grain of the wood and make a lovely, velvety-looking background.

Before you choose a color for your background, place your print against paper or fabric of different colors; your eye will tell you which color sets it off to its best advantage.

COLLECTING YOUR SUPPLIES

Following is a list of the basic supplies you will need before you begin your first decoupage project. Background materials and types of finishes are listed separately, on pages 13 and 14, respectively. You should be able to find everything you need at your local craft shop; if not, try paint and hardware stores for substitutes.

Brayer. This is a soft, rubber roller (the 4-inch size is best) used to flatten prints, roll out excess glue, and roll paper linings flat. You can use a rolling pin, a wallpaper seam roller, a smooth bottle, a glass, or a round pencil in place of a brayer.

Brushes. These are used to apply paint, backgrounds, sealers, and finishes. A ½-inch sable or oxhair brush is excellent for either paint or varnish, though obviously you will need a larger brush if your decoupage object is very big. Be sure to mark your brushes according to their uses—for instance, paint brush or varnish brush—and do not use them interchangeably. Always place your brushes in their proper solvents before they harden. Then clean them, wash them with soap and water, rinse well, and reshape them. (Foam sponge applicators and smooth synthetic sponges may also be used; they are inexpensive, and handy for applying paint, glue, sealer, and even varnish because they do not leave brush strokes.)

Burnisher. This is a 6-inch long, rubber-covered metal tool with one pointed end and one curved end. The burnisher is used to press down the edges of prints after they have been glued. (The bowl end of a stainless steel spoon may be used as a substitute for a burnisher.)

Plasti-tak. This white, puttylike substance holds cuttings temporarily in place while they are being arranged on the object to be decoupaged. (Rubber cement can be used as a substitute.)

Sandpaper. Various grades of sandpaper are used to smooth surfaces between coats of paint or gesso, and for wet sanding between coats of varnish to level prints. Garnet (tan) sandpaper, grades #100 coarse to #240 fine, is best for sanding raw wood. Wet-or-dry sandpaper (black), in grades #400 and #600, is used for wet sanding, and in grade #320 for sanding gesso.

Scissors. Ideally, two pairs of scissors should be used for decoupage: a straight scissors to trim away excess paper from prints, or for straight cutting, and a curved, very sharp cuticle-type scissors with slender points for cutting fine details.

Sealer. Spray or brush-on sealer prevents "bleeding," protects the colors in your prints, strengthens the paper for cutting and gluing, and protects against discoloration by varnish. There are two basic types: *acrylic,* which is thin, and good for sealing prints, paint, wood, and gold braid, and *plastic* (or vinyl), which is heavier, and good for sealing raw wood and tinware. Plastic sealer also keeps metallic liquids and waxes from tarnishing. (Sealer can be made with three parts of shellac to one part alcohol.)

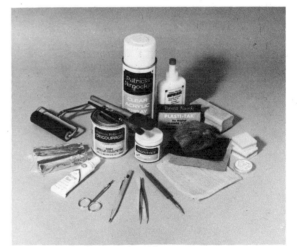

Basic decoupage tools and supplies include spray or brush-on sealer, white glue, Plasti-tak, regular and wet-or-dry sandpaper in various grades, steel wool, a burnisher, scissors, a brayer, and assorted brushes. (See the check lists on page 11 for basic and optional items.)

Solvents. These are used for thinning materials, and for cleaning brushes and removing spills and spots. (See chart below.)

Steel wool. Very fine steel wool (grade #0000 or #000) is used to obtain a satin, rather than a glossy, finish.

Tack cloth. Cheesecloth saturated in varnish is used to remove residue after sanding, and to remove dust between coats of paint or varnish. You can buy tack cloths, or make your own by soaking a piece of cheesecloth in varnish until it feels sticky. (Keep your tack cloth in a tightly-closed jar, or a plastic bag.)

Wax. A fine white furniture paste wax is used to protect the surface of your object after you have finished it. For a high-gloss "piano finish," a mixture of pumice powder and raw linseed oil may be used before waxing.

White glue. A liquid white glue such as Elmer's or Sobo is used to adhere prints to the surface of your object. Decoupage paste or decoupage mucilage may also be used.

SOLVENTS

Material	Thin With:	Clean Up With:
Backgrounds		
gesso	water	water*
metallic wax	turpentine	turpentine
paint:		
acrylic	water	water*
latex	water	soap and water*
oil	turpentine	turpentine or paint remover
wood stains and glazes:		
water base	water	soap and water*
oil base	turpentine	turpentine
Sealers		
acrylic		lacquer thinner
plastic (vinyl)		denatured alcohol
shellac	denatured alcohol	denatured alcohol
Glues		
Acrylic polymer emulsion		water*
decoupage paste or decoupage mucilage		water
white glue	water	water
Finishes		
acrylic		water*
lacquer	lacquer thinner	lacquer thinner
synthetic vinyl		water*
varnish	turpentine	turpentine
Wax		denatured alcohol

* while wet

CHECK LIST OF BASIC SUPPLIES

Brayer

Brushes (or sponge applicators)

Burnisher

Plasti-tak

Sandpaper (garnet and wet-or-dry)

Scissors (curved and straight)

Sealer

Steel wool #0000

Tack cloth

Wax

White glue

Background material (gesso, paint, stain, or metallic wax)

Finish (varnish, lacquer, acrylic, or synthetic)

Solvents (for thinning materials and cleaning brushes)

HOUSEHOLD SUPPLIES

The following items may be useful to you as you decoupage.

Aluminum foil, clear plastic, or brown paper —to cover your work surface

Clean cardboard carton—to invert over your work as a dust cover

Clean cloth—for gluing with brayer

Clear plastic photograph folders—for storing cuttings

Cotton swabs—for cleaning up

Liquid detergent—for wet sanding

Magnifying glass—for very fine work

Paper towels—for cleaning up

Plastic bags—to hold your tack cloths

Plastic gloves—for protection when working with stains and antiquing glazes

Razor blades—for cutting prints through box opening

Ruler or tape measure—for placing hardware and measuring linings

Sponges—for applying paint and cleaning up

Straight pins—to prick bubbles in varnish

Toothpicks—to re-glue edges of prints

White vinegar—for removing glue

OPTIONAL SUPPLIES

Though they are not absolutely necessary, you may want to acquire some of these supplies as you continue with decoupage; other special items are listed where they apply.

Craft knife—for cutting wood and prints

Craft sticks—for stirring paint

Gesso—for smoothing rough wood surfaces

Gold embossed paper braid—for trim

India ink or gold carbon—for your signature

Oil base pencils—for coloring prints and the edges of cutouts

Sanding block—for sanding level surfaces

Sharpener and eraser—for pencils

Tweezers—for picking up small cutouts

Wood filler—for repairs

Glues

Acrylic polymer emulsion—for gluing prints on glass and plastic

Decoupage paste or decoupage mucilage— for thin paper

Thick white glue—for fabric

Hardware

Hinges, hooks, rings, feet, and so on

Awl—to make holes for screws

Screwdriver—for attaching hardware

Linings

Cardboard

Fancy papers, fabrics, and other materials

Special Effects and Bases

Antiquing glazes, liquid leaf, liquid pearl, metallic wax, and so on

Advanced Projects

Hand-moldable epoxy—for repoussé

Gold leaf and sizing—for gilding

Pumice and oil—for polishing to a "piano finish"

Silicone seal adhesive—for three-dimensional work

BACKGROUND MATERIALS

There are many different ways you can treat the background of the object you wish to decoupage. Your choice of a background finish is important, because it will affect how your prints look. For this reason, you should devote some thought to which type of background will set off your print to its best advantage, and experiment, if you can, with the different kinds of background finishes listed here.

Gesso. This is an opaque white liquid that can be used on its own, or as a ground for paint. Gesso is an excellent ground to use on rough or very grainy wood, as it provides a smooth, uniform foundation. Use gesso only if you plan to paint your object; it cannot be used in conjunction with wood stain, since it covers the grain of the wood.

Metallic waxes. These waxes have a transparent, metallic sheen, which allows the grain of the wood to show through. They come in metallic tones such as gold, silver, and copper, and in a large variety of non-metallic colors as well.

Paint. Painting your object will hide the grain of the wood, but it will give you the opportunity to choose almost any color of the rainbow as a background for your prints. Acrylic water base paint is the easiest to use. It comes in many lovely colors (which can be mixed to make still others), is odorless, and dries flat in less than 30 minutes. Latex base indoor paint can also be used. You can use oil base paints if you prefer, but they take much longer to dry and must be thinned with turpentine, so using them is a slower, somewhat messier process.

Wood stains and glazes. Wood stains are excellent to use if your wood object has an attractive grain pattern that you'd like to emphasize. (The grain of the wood will show through the color of the stain.) Stains are available in both oil base and water base form. Oil base stains take from 24 to 48 hours to dry, and can be thinned with turpentine. Water base stains dry in half an hour and can be thinned with water.

If you'd like to stain your wood object with a color you mix yourself, you can make your own wood glaze using turpentine, varnish, and color from a tube of oil paint. Colors such as umber, a rich, dark brown; sienna, a dark, honey tone; and Venetian red, a rusty red, approximate natural wood colors. However, you can make a wood glaze with any color you choose, be it green, yellow, purple, blue, or brown.

(Facing page) Some ideas for personalized projects: a wooden tray decorated as a chess board, a child's stool, a "doghouse purse" for a poodle owner, a wedding invitation framed with three-dimensional decoupage (see page 49), napkin rings, an oval lift-lid jewelry box, a pin, and a pendant. Like the other examples used throughout this book, these unique projects illustrate just a few of the many creative possibilities for decoupage.

FINISHES

Finishes are used after you have applied the print to the object, to protect the print and give the entire object a uniform surface. Whichever finish you choose, always follow the directions on the jar or can carefully.

Acrylic finishes. These water base finishes dry in an hour and can be built up quickly. Unlike other finishes, acrylic finishes are completely colorless—and so are good to use when you're especially interested in keeping your background and print colors from changing. They are excellent for any object that gets constant use, such as a purse, a key ring, or a wastebasket. However, this type of finish water spots easily and is difficult to sand smooth, so it is a good idea to follow finishing with a sanding, a coat or two of varnish, and then a waxing.

Lacquer. Lacquer provides a high-gloss finish that is very attractive. It dries rapidly, but it is less durable than other finishes, so it should be used on objects that are not handled too often, such as wall plaques. Lacquer is not compatible with oil base paint, so be sure to use it only if the background of your object has been painted with a water base paint. Since both lacquer and lacquer thinner give off fumes, use them only in a well-ventilated room.

Synthetic vinyl finishes. This type of finish is water-soluble, dries quickly, and will give the surface of your object a hard, rather plastic look. Following its application with varnishing and wet sanding will make the finish finer and more durable.

Varnish. This is the most widely-used finish for decoupage. It is attractive, strong, and both waterproof and alcohol-proof. It comes in glossy (vinyl) and matte (eggshell) form. Varnish takes from 12 to 24 hours to dry, and is thinned with turpentine. Special decoupage varnish is excellent to use because it does not pull up no matter how many coats you use, and is easier to sand than regular varnish. It gives an exceptionally smooth, deep finish.

Varnish can be applied with a brush or by spraying. Spray varnish is thinner than the brush-on variety and will require more coats; it is a bit more difficult to apply evenly, and so we do not recommend its use.

Buy varnish in small quantities. Once a can of varnish has been opened, it does not keep well for long.

(Facing page) Different finishes create different effects. The speckled yellow box at the back has a lacquer finish. The wedding invitation plaque was stained and varnished (directions for this project are given on pages 16 to 28). Mother of pearl was inlaid over the balloon prints on the hexagonal box, and then finished with a fast synthetic varnish. The orange box (painted black inside) is protected by an acrylic finish and two coats of varnish.

Working With Wood: The Basic Techniques

Now that you are ready to begin a decoupage project, you should be aware of a few general work rules that will help you as you learn the craft. Choose a simple raw wood object, such as a small plaque, for your first project. (White pine and basswood are both good to work on because they are hard and close-grained.) Be sure to keep your first project as simple and inexpensive as possible, because you will be learning the basic techniques as you work.

Keep all your supplies together in a basket or a box so that they are readily available to you, work in as dust-free a room as possible, and use a good, strong lamp so that you do not strain your eyes. Cover your working surface with clear plastic, brown paper, or aluminum foil (do not use newspapers or wax paper). Keep a small notebook with a section for each piece of decoupage you do; list the materials you use, the number of coats of paint, and each coat of finish as you apply it.

Make sure your hands are very clean when you start to work (no hand cream!) and follow the instructions on all the materials you use carefully.

The general instructions given here apply to working on a flat, raw wood surface. Directions for working with old wood, metal, and other materials follow; boxes are discussed on page 29.

PREPARING THE WOOD SURFACE

Sanding. Before you begin sanding, fill in any holes, dents, or cracks in the wood with a wood filler or spackling paste. When the filler or paste has dried, sand it smooth.

Using garnet (tan) sandpaper grades #220 or #240, sand the wood with the grain. (If wood is very rough, start sanding with grades #100 or #120.) When you sand a flat surface, wrap the sandpaper around a sanding block. (You can make a sanding block out of a flat-surfaced block of wood with a piece of felt glued to the bottom.) Keep sanding until the wood feels uniformly smooth. To test, rub with an old stocking, which will catch on any rough spots. Wipe with a tack cloth (see page 17).

Applying gesso (optional). Remember that gesso will cover the grain of the wood; apply it only if you want to cover the grain. Stir the gesso thoroughly and apply it with a soft, damp brush or a damp sponge. Gesso dries in about 30 minutes. Apply at least two coats, one with the grain and one against the grain.

Starting with #320 (black) wet-or-dry sandpaper, and then #400 and #600, dry sand in a circular motion until the surface is smooth. Polish with grade #0000 steel wool (dry) and an old nylon stocking. The gesso should feel satiny to your touch when you finish.

The following photographs show how to make the wedding invitation plaque illustrated on page 15.

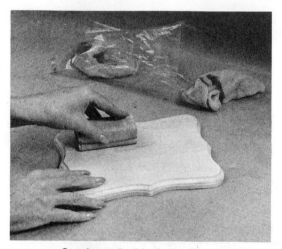

Sand wood *with* the grain.

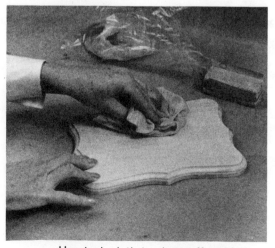

Use tack cloth to clean off residue.

Sealing. Seal wood *before* painting and *after* staining.

So that paint can be applied easily, use plastic or acrylic sealer to seal porous raw wood. One coat of plastic sealer is sufficient, but if you use acrylic sealer, apply two coats.

If you are using a spray, hold the can upright, about 12 inches from your object, and spray on a series of light, misty coats to prevent dripping. If you are using a liquid, apply it with a brush or a sponge applicator.

Seal wood with three coats of sealer before using oil base paints or flat enamels.

APPLYING BACKGROUNDS

Paint. Use a tack cloth (see box) to wipe away dust before you begin to paint. Apply paint lightly and evenly, using a sponge applicator or a soft ½-inch sable or oxhair brush dipped only halfway into the paint. Three coats are usually enough. (A coat of white should be applied first if you are using a transparent color.) Stir the paint thoroughly, and start painting from the middle of your object, working toward the edges. Apply the paint from the unpainted area into the painted one. Wipe off drips with a damp brush. If the paint runs too much, use less paint on your brush. Put your brush in the proper solvent to keep it from drying hard between coats.

If you are mixing a color, make sure you mix only the same kinds of paint—do not mix oil paint with acrylic paint.

After your second coat of paint is thoroughly dry, dry sand it lightly with grade #400 (black) wet-or-dry sandpaper in the direction of the grain until all surfaces are smooth. Wipe with a tack cloth, and apply a third coat of paint.

When the paint is smooth, seal with two light coats of spray sealer or one thin coat of brush-on sealer to keep it clean while you arrange your design.

Stains. Sand but *do not seal* the wood before you use a stain. Apply stain with a cloth, a sponge applicator, or a brush, going with the grain of the wood. (It is wise to protect your hands with rubber gloves when applying stains.) Apply the stain heavily for a dark color, and more lightly for a lighter tone. Wipe off excess with a cloth or paper towel.

Allow the stain to dry, rub it with your tack cloth, and then apply a coat of sealer. If you wish to remove a stain, use the proper solvent and then seal with plastic sealer. Whichever stain you use, follow the directions on the container carefully.

Metallic waxes. These waxes, which have a metallic sheen, color the wood while allowing the grain to show through. Using a brush or a sponge applicator, dip lightly into turpentine, then into the metallic wax; work the wax into the wood, going with the grain. The more turpentine you use, the lighter the color you will get. Allow 1 hour drying time, and then buff with a soft cloth. Seal with plastic (vinyl) sealer.

Apply stain with smooth, even strokes.

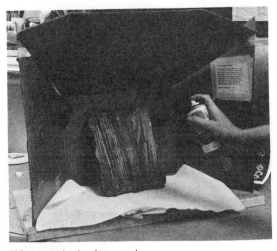

When stain is dry, seal.

PREPARING YOUR PRINTS

It is best to start with a fairly simple print on thin, non-glossy paper which is blank on the wrong side. (Be sure your paper isn't *too* thin. If it is, it may wrinkle, or the glue may show through.)

Coloring. Study your print carefully before you color it. Colors can be brightened, softened, or changed to different tones if desired. Use oil base pencils, and color (or erase colors) to your taste. For easier cutting, thicken very thin lines, such as fine stems, butterfly antennae, and so on, with a pencil the same color as the print.

Sealing. Prints are sealed to keep colors from running, to strengthen the paper so that it doesn't tear, and to prevent the paper from stretching when it is wet.

Spray your print with two light coats of plastic sealer or three light coats of acrylic spray, holding the can approximately 12 inches away from the print. If you use a liquid sealer, pat it on very lightly with a sponge.

Note: If you want to use a print with writing on the back, seal both back and front with two light coats of acrylic sealer. If the writing does not show through to the front, paint the back with white paint (if you are using a light background) or black paint (if your background color is dark). If the writing *does* show through, do not use the print.

Thinning heavy papers. Extremely heavy papers, such as postcards and some greeting cards, must be thinned before they can be used for decoupage.

Apply a coat of white glue to the back of the paper, and let it dry for approximately 20 minutes. Starting from a corner, begin peeling the paper away. (You can roll it around a pencil as you peel it off.) Then sand the back of the paper with very fine sandpaper for an even surface. (Again, be careful not to thin paper too much.)

To transfer prints, see page 55.

CUTTING YOUR PRINTS

Before you actually cut your print, practice cutting out magazine pictures. Use a sharp, curved scissors with narrow points, such as a cuticle scissors.

Hold the scissors with your thumb and middle finger, and rest the blade on your index finger. This supports and steadies your scissors and will guide the cutting. The points of the scissors should be turned away from the paper, and your palm should face up, so that the scissors are tilted to bevel the edge of the paper. Use your other hand to feed and turn the paper into the scissors as you cut. Hold the print rather loosely, so it moves easily as you cut along the lines of the picture. Always hold the bulk of the paper in your other hand, away from the point of the scissors.

Remove excess paper from the outside of your print with straight scissors. (All straight lines should be cut with straight scissors.)

Start cutting from the inside, so that you can hold onto the outer

Spray upright print with sealer.

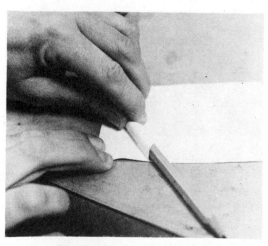
Thinning a heavy paper

CUTTING PRINTS

Use straight scissors to remove extra paper, and then cut print into smaller sections for easier handling.

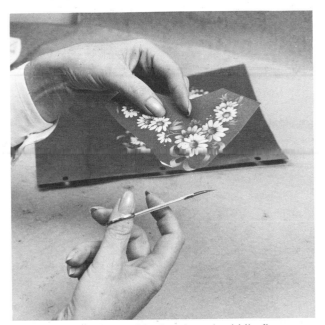

Hold curved scissors with thumb and middle finger, using index finger to support and guide the scissors.

Always face the point of the curved scissors *away* from the print to be cut. Keep the part you are cutting to the left of the scissors.

To cut a small inner section, first poke a hole through the top of the paper. Then cut with tips of scissors coming up from *underneath* the paper, as illustrated here.

Singe edges of invitation; remove excess burnt paper carefully.

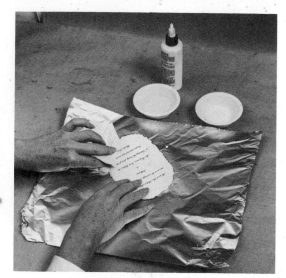

Then coat front and back of invitation with acrylic polymer emulsion (see box on page 18).

edges of the paper during the entire cutting process. Cut from underneath so that your hands and scissors do not block your view of the print. (Only the tips of the scissors should be visible.)

To cut a small inner section, poke a hole with the point of your scissors through the paper from the top. Then make a small cut from the hole so your scissors can cut (not tear) from underneath. Then work the scissors through the hole from underneath and cut.

Cut the outside areas last.

Ladders. If your print has fragile tendrils or other delicate details that might break off while you cut, draw ladders (parallel pencil lines) to attach these sections to the rest of the print. Leave the ladders on while you cut, as they help to keep the print together. Cut them off before you glue. (If pieces of your print break, or are accidentally cut off, they can be put back together when you glue them down; the breaks will not be noticeable.)

Serrated edges, which glue down somewhat better than straight edges, look softer than long, straight lines. To obtain a serrated edge, wiggle the paper back and forth gently as you cut.

Try for a variety of cutting techniques to make your designs more interesting. You can change, improve, and exaggerate shapes with your scissors. Think in terms of textures as you cut—round the edges of petals, serrate the edges of feathers and fur, and so on.

If you are not sure you have cut a good shape, turn the piece over and look at the blank side. Looking at this abstract shape will help your eye to judge whether your curves need more shape or your lines are too sharp.

Note: A sharp, pointed knife is useful for cutting sharp corners, angles, stairs, or small slits. When cutting with a knife, place your print on a piece of glass and cut at an angle so the edges are beveled.

After cutting, place your cutouts on a black paper background and color in all the white edges with the appropriate pencil colors. *Reseal.* To spray cutouts, put them in a box so they won't fly around. Then put them in an envelope or folder so they won't be mislaid.

COMPOSING YOUR DESIGN

One of the most exciting aspects of decoupage is the composition, or arrangement, of the prints on the object. First, arrange your cuttings temporarily with Plasti-tak, moving and rearranging them until the entire composition pleases you. Do not glue them down (see page 23) until you are completely satisfied with how they look. Try moving a few feet away from the design and looking at it—then turn it around and examine your design from all angles. Piece and re-piece it, trim it and reshape it until it is perfect. A good starting point is the main section or the largest piece of the print—then work around it with smaller pieces. Make sure that all the colors and pieces are harmonious, and that all the materials are suited to each other. Draw on your growing awareness of shapes and colors to achieve a pleasing rhythm of design and color.

(Left) The print that wraps all around this pert flower purse was cut out only at the top, and a few pieces were glued to the lid. Gold braid, painted white to match the background, was added around the bottom as a "fence." (Below) Botanical flower prints create another effect on the white Shaker box purse here. The ivory tissue cover displays a different owl print on each side. Metallic wax was used for the sapphire blue background on the distinctive evening purse. The lid opens on a single hinge to reveal a blue velvet lining and a tiny mirror (see page 33).

Hardware. If your project requires the use of hardware, such as hinges, a clasp, or a handle, select it before you arrange your composition. Mark the spaces that will be taken up by hardware so that it will not interfere with the placement of your print. (For instructions on installing hardware, see page 32.)

Trim. If you decide to use gold braid or paper borders, make sure that they are appropriate for your prints, and that they look good with the colors you'll be using.

Seal any gold braid you use with three coats of acrylic sealer to prevent tarnishing. You can silver it by wiping it with nail polish remover or lacquer thinner. Or you can antique it by rubbing a stain or an antiquing glaze over it after you have sealed it. You can paint gold braid so that it matches the background color of your project, or so that it contrasts in color. Always reseal after you stain or paint, and have the braid ready before you glue your print.

Antique white and ivory are popular background colors for both traditional and contemporary prints.

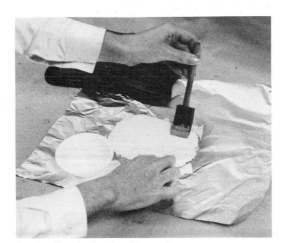
Apply glue to back of invitation.

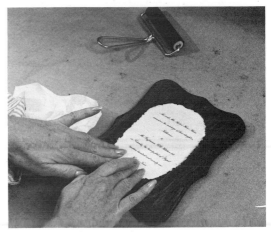
Position carefully on plaque.

GLUING

A liquid white glue (which dries transparent) is most often used in decoupage, though decoupage paste or decoupage mucilage may be used as well. Decoupage paste and mucilage dry more slowly than white glue, so prints can be moved around over a longer period of time. They are well worth using if you are working with exceptionally thin paper or very delicate cutouts.

Glue and paste can be mixed in equal quantities, or you can add a few drops of water for a lighter glue.

Materials

white glue, decoupage paste or decoupage mucilage

brayer (a round glass or a rolling pin will do)

lint-free cloth

dish of water

sponges

paper towels

burnisher

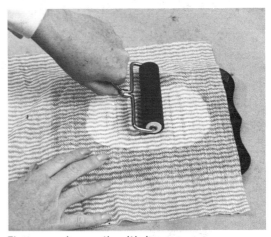
Flatten and smooth with brayer.

Before you glue, remove the Plasti-tak from each print cutout and the surface of your object by rubbing lightly with a small ball of Plasti-tak. Mark the object lightly with pencil just under the edges of each print piece so that you can reposition it accurately.

Start by gluing the largest pieces first, then the smaller cutouts. Coat the entire back surface of each piece lightly and evenly (use your fingers or a brush). The entire piece must be covered with glue or the print will pop up after finishing. Do not overlap pieces, but cut to fit them together so that they just touch. (If you overlap edges, you will need more coats of finish.) When gluing very delicate pieces, apply glue to the object, rather than the paper.

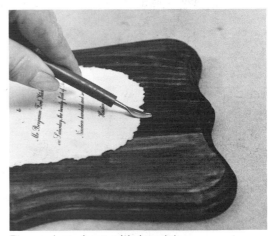
Press edges down with burnisher.

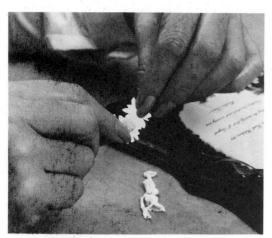

Use Plasti-tak to arrange prints.

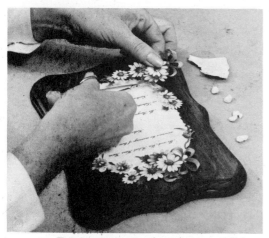

Trim cutouts so they don't overlap.

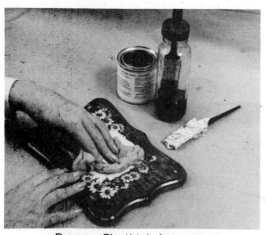

Remove Plasti-tak from one cutout at a time, apply glue, and press down.

After you have glued a piece into position, place a slightly damp cloth (well wrung out) over it and roll over the cloth with a brayer, moving from the center of the piece to the edges. Remove the cloth. Then, using the flat of your finger in a rolling motion, press down again from the center to the outside edges. Wipe away excess glue immediately with a damp, well wrung out sponge.

If you are gluing a large print that does not have many sections cut out of it, use a sharp knife to make slits at lines in each area of the print so that glue can escape from under it. Apply glue generously to object with a soft brush or a sponge, and then roll over it carefully with your brayer. Continue as with small pieces.

Burnishing. When glue is dry, gently press down the edges of each print piece with the curved end of a burnisher. This will flatten the edges and ensure that they are glued down well.

Check all edges and apply more glue if necessary, using a toothpick or a pin, and reburnish. If you have difficulty removing any glue spots with water, use a cotton swab and a mixture of warm water and white vinegar. Be sure to remove *all* excess glue.

Let the glue dry overnight before you apply a finish.

Applying trim. If you are using gold braid as a trim, measure one piece to go around your object. Put glue on the surface of the object where the braid will go, and allow the glue to get tacky. Put glue on back of braid and position it carefully; then roll it and burnish it.

To miter corners, let two edges of braid overlap, and then make a diagonal cut with a straight scissors (see diagram below).

Position braid on box and glue sides. At corners, cut braid with scissors before gluing it down.

FINISHING

The following rules apply to all decoupage finishes.

1. Use a tack cloth before each coat of finish.

2. Never mix products or brands of finishes unless you are *absolutely certain* that they are compatible.

3. Use different brushes for finishes with different solvents.

4. Place your brush or applicator into the proper solvent immediately after using it.

5. Apply your finish to a level, horizontal surface.

6. Prop the object on a clean can or a jar to dry.

7. Place a clean carton over the object after finishing to keep dust off it. (Make air holes in the sides of the carton.)

8. Before applying the next coat of finish, press your thumb hard on the surface. If it leaves a print, the finish isn't dry. Wait.

9. Don't varnish on wet or humid days—humidity lengthens drying time.

10. Apply two or three coats of finish to the insides of boxes or the backs of plaques to prevent wood from warping.

11. Allow the finish to cure, or fully harden, for several weeks before using your object.

12. Always read the instructions on finish containers. They will advise drying time, the best brush to use, and the appropriate solvent for the particular product you are using. Follow all directions carefully (and add extra drying time to be on the safe side!).

The transparent coatings of a finish must be built up layer by layer to protect the piece of decoupage and to achieve a beautiful, durable finish for your work. Fewer coats will result in a sculptural (raised) look; many coats are necessary to level the print for a flat surface so you cannot feel the paper beneath.

Materials

finish and solvent

brush

tack cloth

two glass jars

clothespin

Varnish

There are two types of decoupage varnish, and each gives a different finish. The clear, glossy (vinyl) type looks shiny when it dries, but can be polished down to a matte satin look. The matte, low luster (eggshell) type diffuses color and dries to a mellow amber, giving an antique-looking finish. These varnishes can be used together: If you want only a slightly amber finish, you can build up coats of glossy vinyl varnish, and then use matte eggshell varnish for the final coats. (If you can't find a decoupage varnish, use a clear furniture varnish.)

CARE OF BRUSHES

Take a glass (*not* plastic) jar with a tight-fitting metal cover, make a hole in the center large enough for the brush handle, and fill jar with enough solvent to cover the bristles. Suspend brush in the solvent by holding it up with a clothespin so the bristles don't touch the bottom.

Always have a second jar of clean solvent handy. When you are ready to use your brush, dip it in the solvent and swish it around. Squeeze brush with your fingers to remove any excess solvent.

You can store a finish-laden brush (or sponge applicator) by wrapping it in foil and putting it in the freezer. (Eventually, of course, you must clean brushes and applicators in the proper solvent.)

When storing brushes that are not in use, wash them in warm water and soap, rinse, reshape, and then wrap in foil. Do not wash sponge applicators after they have been cleaned with denatured alcohol or lacquer thinner; simply clean with solvent and wrap in foil.

Remember: Never mix brushes for sealer, paint, varnish, and lacquer! Always use different brushes for materials that require different solvents.

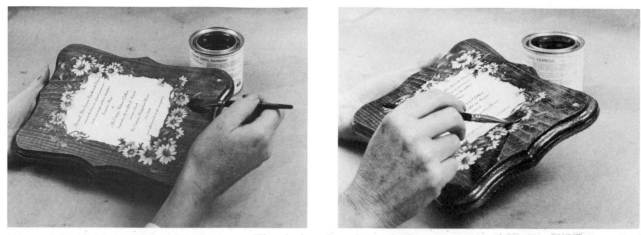

(Above left) Apply varnish *with* the grain of the wood. (Above right) Then brush *against* the grain to force out air bubbles. Finish by holding brush almost horizontal; with tip, remove last air bubbles. (Directions for wet sanding and for polishing are given on page 28.)

The drying time for varnish is approximately 12 to 24 hours. (Labels frequently underestimate the drying time that is necessary because of the buildup of many coats.)

Before you choose a varnish, test various types to see how they look. Put several coats on a piece of glass, and then hold the glass over your project; this will give you a rough idea of how the varnish will look on your project (the color in the varnish will affect your paint and print colors).

Apply varnish in thin, even coats to avoid streaking, using a ½-inch sable or oxhair brush. Thin varnish with turpentine as needed. Always close varnish cans as tightly as possible. If a skin forms on the top, remove it before you start to work.

To apply. Dip your brush halfway into the varnish. Holding it at a 45 degree angle, "scrub" in the varnish, beginning on the background and then moving onto the print. Work from the center of the object to the edges, picking up your brush at the edges to prevent "rollover" (an accumulation of excess varnish). Then brush in long strokes with the grain until there is no more varnish in the brush.

To force out air bubbles, brush *against* the grain, holding the brush at an angle. Then shorten up on the handle and hold the brush almost horizontally. With the tip, brush lightly *with* the grain to smooth out any remaining air bubbles. Continue working from an unvarnished section into a varnished one. (Prick stubborn bubbles with a pin, and smooth over with your brush.)

When the first coat of varnish is finished, prop your object up on a clean jar or a can to dry. (Sunlight, heat from an electric light bulb, or a blower-type hair dryer will speed up drying time.)

Repeat this process at least ten times, letting each coat of varnish dry thoroughly before you start on the next. (Two or three coats of varnish are sufficient for the lips and liners of boxes.)

Between coats, wrap brush in foil and store in freezer (or suspend in a jar of solvent; see box on page 25).

Wet sanding. After a minimum of ten coats of varnish have been applied, you are ready to wet sand for the first time (directions for wet sanding are given on page 28). After wet sanding, wash your object and dry it thoroughly. (It will have a moire taffeta look, but this will disappear with the next coat of varnish.)

Continue to build up coats of varnish and to wet sand between every three to five coats until you have obtained a satisfactory finish. If your print is on thick paper, it will require more coats of varnish than thin paper would. If you want your print to be completely buried in varnish, add a few extra coats to allow for the fact that varnish shrinks as it cures.

When you are satisfied with the finish, wet sand with #600 (black) wet-or-dry sandpaper. For a very shiny finish, apply a final coat or two of varnish especially carefully and then polish (see page 28).

Lacquer

Lacquer gives a high gloss finish, and since it dries rapidly, it can be applied more frequently than varnish. However, it is not as durable; it is more susceptible to extremes in temperature and will crack more readily than varnish. In addition, it is not compatible with oil base paint or flat enamel, and has a tendency to make prints "bleed" (be sure to seal your prints very carefully if you plan to use lacquer). Nevertheless, it does produce a beautiful finish quickly when properly applied.

The drying time for lacquers varies from 1 to 6 hours; read the label on your container.

Because it dries rapidly, lacquer should be flowed on, not "scrubbed in" as varnish is. Otherwise, apply as you would varnish. Do not begin to wet sand (see page 28) until you have built up a minimum of ten coats. Continue as with varnish.

Acrylic Finishes

These water base finishes dry very rapidly and can be applied every hour, with either a soft brush or a sponge applicator. Apply in one direction, as brushing this type of finish back and forth will cause bubbles to appear. Clean applicator with water.

After several coats, wet sand (see page 28), wash off, dry, and then apply several coats of varnish for an especially hard, durable surface. This will also make it waterproof and alcohol-proof. Then polish (see page 28).

Synthetic Vinyl Finishes

These produce a hard, plastic-looking finish. They are quick-drying and can be applied every 20 minutes with a brush or a sponge applicator. Apply at least two coats of varnish and wet sand for a finer, stronger finish, and to make it waterproof and alcohol-proof. Polish (see page 28).

Finish problems. If you have drips, sags, or runs you are using too much finish. Use a brush dipped in the appropriate solvent to remove them. (Large globs can be sliced off with a sharp knife.)

If your finish cracks or puckers, it is because the preceding coat was not thoroughly dry. Let your object dry out for a day or two, and wrinkles will eventually disappear after the next coat is applied.

If your object gets dropped or picks up lint, wipe it off with denatured alcohol.

Dip wet-or-dry sandpaper in sudsy water, and sand in a back and forth motion *with* the grain.

WET SANDING

Wet sanding is an important step in finishing your object; it removes air bubbles and foreign matter and brings the surface of the wood even with the surface of the print.

Materials

dish of soapy water (use liquid dish-washing detergent)

grade #400 (black) wet-or-dry sandpaper

sponge

paper towels or a clean cloth

Wrap a small piece of sandpaper around a sponge, dip it into soapy water, and work back and forth in the direction of the grain. Work lightly over the print area, making sure you don't sand through to the print. (If you do, recolor it with oil base pencil; touch up paint with paint and a fine brush, and reseal carefully.) With a damp cloth or paper towel, wipe off any white residue that forms as you continue to wet sand. Rinse off soap and dry with a soft towel.

POLISHING

Waxing is necessary to protect the surface of your object after you have finished it. Waxing should be repeated every six months.

Materials

2 soft, lint-free cloths

white furniture paste wax

grade #0000 steel wool

old nylon stocking

pumice and finishing oil (optional)

Matte or satiny finish. Rub your project in one direction with a small piece of #0000 steel wool until all the shiny spots have been eliminated and your object looks very dull. (Wrap steel wool around a cotton swab to remove difficult-to-reach spots.)

Wash off and dry your object, and rub it hard with an old nylon stocking. Then apply a small amount of white furniture wax with a soft, lint-free cloth. Rub the wax into the surface and polish with a soft, dry cloth.

Shiny finish. For a high-gloss "piano finish," mix pumice (an abrasive powder) with a finishing oil—lemon or linseed—to a syrupy consistency. (Rottenstone may be used instead of pumice.) Polish briskly with a soft cloth or a felt pad, working with the grain of the wood. Wipe away excess oil, dry with a soft cloth, and wax as above.

Rub with very fine steel wool, wax, and then polish with a soft cloth.

Boxes

When you work on a box, you will be working with at least four sides, a top surface, and an interior as well. Each of these areas should be done with care, as you can be sure that admirers will want to examine your work both inside and out. Some may even turn the box over, and so you might want to plan a nice surprise for the bottom, too—perhaps a butterfly, or some other cutout appropriate to your design. For the perfect finishing touch, you can add your signature and the date (use India ink or gold carbon).

Following are some hints and procedures that apply to boxes; for the basic steps involved in preparing raw wood, sanding and sealing it, and applying backgrounds, see the section on Working With Wood: The Basic Techniques.

First, remove any excess glue from the inside of your box with a craft knife, the pointed end of a burnisher, or a small wood chisel. If you gouge out any wood in the process, fill in with wood filler or spackling paste, and then sand smooth.

Do not round the corners and edges of the box while sanding. Use an emery board, or a piece of sandpaper wrapped around a stick, to reach inside corners. Stop sanding when every surface you feel is smooth and even. Wipe with a tack cloth before sealing.

Set-in lids. If your box has a set-in lid, it will not need hinges. Sand the insides of the box until the top fits so loosely that it wiggles in both directions when the box is closed—this will allow for the coats of paint and finish you will apply.

Lift lids. Lift-lid boxes have removable liners and do not require hinges. Remove and sand the liners and the insides of the box. Replace the liners, put on the cover, and see that it fits very loosely. Then remove the liners and paint and finish them separately. When all pieces of the box have been finished, glue them in.

Cutting wood for recessed hinges (optional). If you are planning to use recessed hinges, you must cut out spaces for them before painting or staining your box.

Since most small hinges are ⅛ inch in depth when closed flat, you will need to cut 1⁄16 inch from both the top and bottom lips of the box to accommodate them. The width of the hinge must be the same size or smaller than the flat lip of the box or the hinge will protrude.

Place the two closed hinges on the flat lip of the bottom half of the box. Measure equally from both outside corners of the box, and make pencil marks around the half sides of the hinges where you want them to go. Cut the wood down inside these pencil marks 1⁄16 inch with a very sharp craft knife or a single-edge razor blade. Slice carefully, making as flat a surface as you can where you cut, and sand the recesses smooth with an emery board. Then repeat this procedure on the top of the box.

Put the lid on the box, slip the hinges in place, and make sure they fit quite loosely to allow for the buildup of paint and finish.

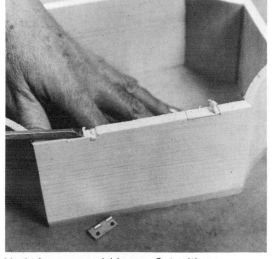

Mark for recessed hinges. Cut with a craft knife; remove wood with a chisel.

If wood is rough or very grainy, use gesso before painting. Apply gesso as smoothly as possible, alternating each coat with and against the grain. Then polish with steel wool.

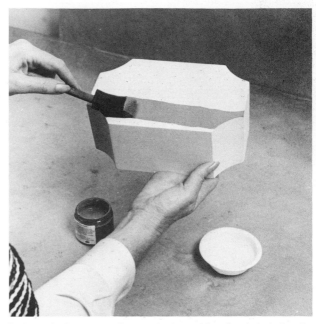

Start painting away from edge, working back to edge to avoid drips. Always work from an unpainted area into a painted one. Smooth, even coats are essential for a good foundation.

Prop objects on jars or cans to dry. Cover with an inverted carton (with air holes cut in sides) to prevent dust from settling on wet paint or varnish.

Remove and set aside until the box has been finished. (For instructions on installing hinges, see page 32.)

Outside hinges are applied after the box has been finished (see instructions on page 32).

Painting. Holding the box from the inside with your other hand, paint one side at a time, turning the box to keep the working surface horizontal. Then paint the top of your box if it has a lid.

Place the box upside down on a jar or a can to dry.

Paint the bottom part of your box, and then dry in the same manner.

When dry, apply at least two coats of paint to the insides of the top and bottom of the box. Apply two very light coats of paint to the lips of the box.

Gluing. If parts of your design are to be glued over the box opening, hold the box closed with masking tape, glue the print down, and when thoroughly dry, cut through print at the opening with a razor or a craft knife. Remove masking tape and check the edges of the print to see if they need additional glue. Color white edges.

Finishing. Apply varnish (or other finish) in the same manner as paint, holding and turning the box so that your work surface is horizontal. Apply two or three coats of finish to the insides of the box to prevent the wood from warping. Apply two or three coats to the lips of the box so it will close evenly.

The scale of a print must work in harmony with the size and shape of the box. Note the variety of background colors, types of prints, and composition of designs enhancing the various box shapes here. Real stamps were used on the red box in the foreground.

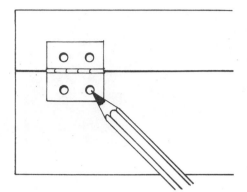

Holding hinge in place with your finger, mark pencil dots in the holes of the hinge.

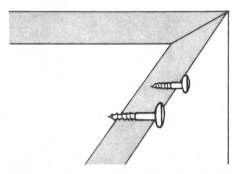

Place screws on lip of box to check that they do not extend past the inside edge of the lip.

Use a very small screwdriver to install screws for recessed hinges.

HARDWARE

Hardware, such as ball feet, claw feet, rings, or knobs, can be both functional and decorative. Choose your hardware to enhance the style, size, and shape of your box. Solid brass hardware, although it is slightly more costly than pressed brass, is better to use. It can be painted, antiqued, and sealed, or it can be painted black and then silvered. Hardware should be installed last, after finishing and polishing your project.

Materials

small awl or ice pick

wire cutter

small screwdriver

cake of soap

ruler

white glue

masking tape

To install hardware, first check the length of your screws against the depth of the wood of your box to make sure the screws are not too long. If they are, clip their ends with a wire cutter (or use shorter screws).

Start the holes for your screws with an awl or an ice pick to make sure you don't split the wood, and roll your screws in a cake of soap so they will enter the wood smoothly. Dip very thin screws or nails into glue before you install them.

Hardware for other items, such as a decorative hanging ring for a plaque, should be installed in the same manner.

Outside hinges. Fasten the top and bottom of your box together with masking tape. Measure in equidistantly from the back edges of the box for placement, line up the cylinders on the hinges with the opening of the box, and then mark lightly with pencil. Place the hinges on the back of the box and mark all the holes for screws with pencil. Start these holes with an awl and then insert the screws (first rolled in soap) with a small screwdriver.

Recessed hinges. Place the hinges in the spaces cut out for them (see page 29). Mark the holes for screws on the bottom lip first. Then proceed as above.

LININGS

A lining adds the finishing touch to any decoupaged object. There are many suitable materials for linings—paper, including wrapping paper, tea paper, foils, and marbled paper; and fabrics, including felt, burlap, velvet, and cotton. Your choice of lining should be the result of practical as well as aesthetic considerations—for instance, a jewelry box would need a soft, rather thick lining, while a purse would need a durable, sturdy one.

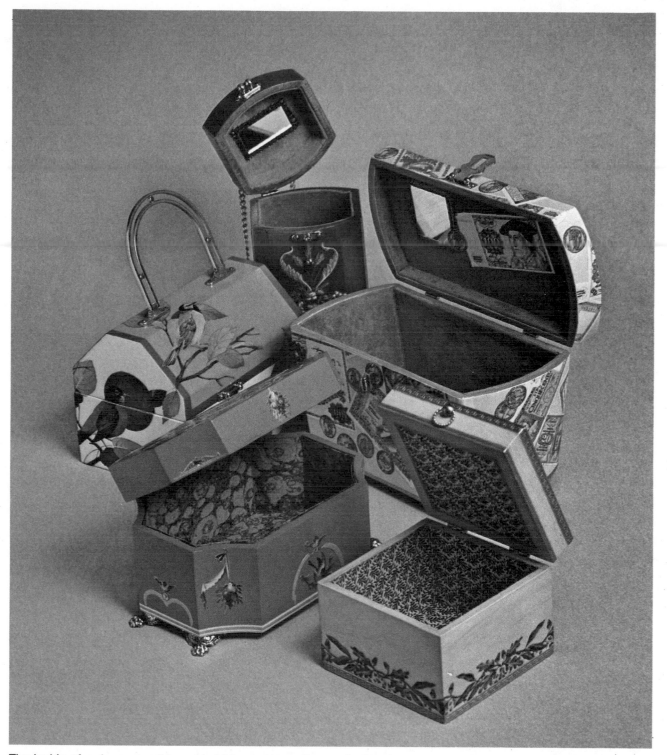

The inside of a decoupaged box should be as interesting and attractive as the outside. The inside of the blue purse is lined with velvet, and holds a tiny gold-braided mirror. The "money purse" carries the design from the outside into the lid, where the motif is balanced by a mirror. Notice the effective positioning of the bird, which appears to be entering the birdhouse purse on the left. Marbled paper lines the terra-cotta box, and Italian endpaper enhances the square box in the foreground. Appropriate hardware further complements these handsome boxes.

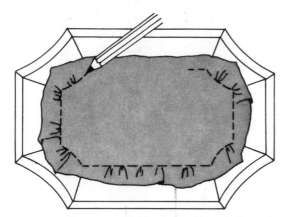

For unusual shapes, place and mark paper towel inside box. Trim to fit and transfer pattern to cardboard.

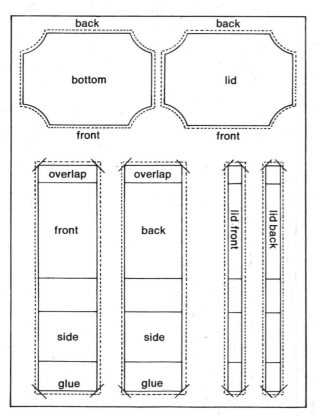

Lay out all cardboard patterns on lining, allowing an extra ¼″ border around each piece before cutting.

Materials

white glue

acrylic sealer

straight scissors

pliable cardboard or manila file folders

paper or fabric for lining

ruler or tape measure

Preparation. Seal lining paper on both sides with three coats of acrylic sealer. Fabrics, except velvet or similar piled fabrics, should be sealed on the front only. (But test a scrap first, to be sure the sealer you're using does not spot the fabric.)

Patterns. Paper and fabric linings can be glued directly to the inside of a box, but it is preferable to glue your paper or fabric to cardboard patterns, and then to glue these units into the box. .

First take the inside measurements from one side of your box to the opposite side, all the way around. Then measure the depth of the sides from the inside lip to the bottom of the box. Make separate patterns for the bottom and the top of the box.

If your paper or fabric will crease crisply in the corners, you can make a pattern for the sides in one continuous strip the exact length and depth of all four sides. Score back of cardboard at the corners. Crease the corners with a ruler.

If your fabric or paper will not crease sharply, make individual cardboard patterns for the top and bottom and for each side.

After you have cut your patterns, lay them down on your fabric or paper, and cut, adding a ¼-inch border all around that will be glued down to the back of the cardboard.

Cut all four corners diagonally so that the lining will lie flat when you turn the ¼-inch borders over the back.

Place the cardboard on the wrong side of the fabric or paper. Put an even coat of glue on the ¼-inch pattern border and glue to back of cardboard. Press down with burnisher.

Coat the sides and bottom of the box with glue. Insert the sides first. Glue in the bottom last, and then continue with the top of the box in the same way.

Other ideas: A stunning lining can be made by cutting irregular circles or ovals from gold or silver tea paper or foil. Fold the paper in 1-inch accordion pleats and cut through several layers at a time. Glue the ovals or circles in an overlapping pattern and press down with burnisher. They can then be sealed and/or antiqued.

You can paint the inside in a contrasting color, or use metallic paint, and/or add decoupage to the inside, adding your signature and the date as a final touch (use India ink or gold carbon).

Put felt on the bottom of your box so it won't scratch the table. A plaque can be backed with fabric or paper.

Working With Old Wood

If you decide to decoupage an old wood object that has already been varnished, you must remove the old finish before you begin. Use a commercial varnish remover, sand, wipe the wood with denatured alcohol, and then seal as you would raw wood (see page 17).

If your object is painted wood in good condition, sand, clean with denatured alcohol, and seal.

If your object is covered with heavy, lumpy, or chipped paint, scrape it down and then remove the paint with a commercial paint remover. Sand, wipe with denatured alcohol, and seal.

Wood that has been stained or oiled should be wiped off with turpentine and sanded lightly.

Remove old wax with #0000 steel wool and then wipe with denatured alcohol and seal.

If you must make repairs on old wood, use wood filler and then sand it. Wood that is terribly uneven or damaged can be greatly improved with wood filler or spackling paste, and then several coats of gesso, followed by sanding, sealing, and painting.

Once old wood has been prepared for finishing as indicated here, follow the directions for Working With Wood: The Basic Techniques.

Working With Metal, New and Old

New metal. Clean new metal (except galvanized metal) with denatured alcohol and cover it with one coat of a metal primer. This will dry in 24 hours. Then proceed as with raw wood. (See the section on Working With Wood: The Basic Steps.)

Wash galvanized metal with a solution of one part warm water to one part vinegar, dry thoroughly, and sand lightly. Clean with a tack cloth and then proceed as with raw wood.

Old metal. Remove any rust with sandpaper and steel wool, and remove any finish with a commercial solvent. Hammer out any dents, then clean with denatured alcohol, sand, and apply a metal primer.

If your metal object is covered with paint that is in good condition, clean it with denatured alcohol, sand lightly, clean with a tack cloth, and repaint.

A handsome tole tray is pictured on page 37.

Working With Glass

An early form of decoupage was *potichomania*—revived in the nineteenth-century fad for imitating old Chinese painted porcelain ware by coating the inside of glass vessels with colored cutouts or prints. Decoupage inside or under glass is a much faster process than working on a wooden surface. Projects such as flat plates, ashtrays, switch plates, vases, bowls, ginger jars, and lamps can often be completed in just a few days.

If your project is transparent glass (or plastic) you can decoupage either the outside, the inside, or both; if it is opaque glass (or a similar material—ceramic or plastic, for example), you can work on the outside as you would on wood.

Plastic and plexiglass projects require the same materials and make use of the same techniques as glass projects. The only glue to use with synthetic objects is acrylic polymer emulsion.

Save a few empty glass jars and use them to practice various background techniques and to test different products before you begin new projects.

DECOUPAGE OVER GLASS

Doing decoupage on the outside of glass, ceramic, or plastic is very similar to the process of doing decoupage on wood. The steps involved are: **1.** cleaning the surface thoroughly; **2.** applying a coat of plastic sealer or acrylic polymer emulsion; **3.** painting or gessoing the background; and **4.** continuing as with wood.

At an art gallery in Nassau we saw a ten-gallon water jug for sale that had been painted and then decorated with picture cutouts. The artist had painted some of the edges of the paper and then lacquered over them. The jug was large, attractive—and quite costly. The same artist had even decorated broken jugs, covering the jagged edges with candle wax. She had, in effect, created a new form of decoupaged sculpture!

You might try using decoupage over the glass of old wine bottles to make candleholders or vases. Or use a large jar to make a terrarium, and decorate it with mushroom prints, butterflies, or tiny mice or frogs.

STEP-BY-STEP DECOUPAGE OVER GLASS

1. Seal front of print and cut out.
2. Clean surface of glass.
3. Coat glass with sealer.
4. Apply background.
5. Compose and glue cutouts.
6. Apply finish; then polish.

This Christmas plate for 1974 features a cartouche, or frame, of roses and embossed gold letters. The red center was painted, and the rest of the glass plate was gilded with Dutch metal (see page 56). The back was finished in marbled leaf and then varnished.

The tole tray here, with its insects and carniverous flowering plants, is an example of the combination of contemporary and traditional materials. The vibrant colors are quite effective against the black background.

Various background treatments are possible when you decoupage under glass. In the examples here, black paint makes a striking background for the Oriental prints used on the lamp in the foreground. Sand, instead of paint, was used to create a background for the seashell lamp behind it. A coat of varnish was brushed over the interior of the glass, and loose sand was then rolled around the inside until it adhered firmly to the surface. (For other background treatments, see pages 41–43.)

DECOUPAGE UNDER GLASS

Most decoupage with glass is done from underneath, because the glass acts as a substitute for the many coats of finish that would be necessary otherwise. The process of doing decoupage under glass is the reverse of working with wood, as you are working from front to back. The steps are: **1.** sealing the print on the back before cutting; **2.** arranging the composition; **3.** gluing cutouts under cleaned glass; **4.** sealing the glass surface; and **5.** applying the background.

For your first project, pick something with a flat surface, such as a switch plate or a flat dish.

Materials

acrylic polymer emulsion (or decoupage mucilage; see note on page 40)

sealer (optional)

plain paper

china marking pencil (not white) or crayon

synthetic sponge or foam rubber

lint-free cloth and/or disposable honeycomb cloth

denatured alcohol

background materials—paint, gesso, paper, felt, and so on

bowl of water

varnish

felt (optional)

Preparation. You can use a thick print under glass, but if it has a slick, coated surface it will be difficult to glue. Seal the back of the print with acrylic emulsion (or sealer) before cutting. (Do not seal the front unless it is a hand-colored print.) Try to use rather small cutouts, because the acrylic emulsion dries very quickly. If you do use a large cutout (more than 2 inches in diameter), slit it in various places with a razor blade or a craft knife so you can force air bubbles out. Make the slits where they will show the least (preferably, on a line). Keep all the pieces in a plastic bag so that you don't lose them.

Composition. Make a template (paper pattern) of your glass object by placing it on a piece of plain paper and tracing around it with a pencil. Then, arrange your cutouts on top of this pattern to see how they look. Take your time, and keep moving your prints around until you are entirely satisfied with your composition. When you are pleased with it, lower the glass onto the pattern and trace the outlines of the pieces onto the front of the glass with a china marker. If there are many pieces, it may help if you number each print piece on the back with a pencil and number its corresponding outline on the front surface of the glass with the marker.

Cleaning the glass. Wash off the back of the glass with soap and water and rinse it thoroughly. Use vinegar or ammonia to remove any grease, and dry with a lint-free cloth. Lift the glass by the sides or

---

STEP-BY-STEP DECOUPAGE UNDER GLASS

1. Seal back of print and cut out.
2. Arrange composition and mark front of glass with china marker.
3. Clean back of glass surface.
4. Glue print to back of glass; remove excess glue.
5. Seal entire back of glass surface.
6. Apply background; seal when dry.
7. Varnish.

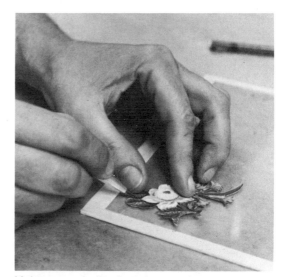

Make several slits in a large print before gluing. (When cutting with a knife, place the print on a piece of glass.)

with a cloth to keep it free of fingerprints, and place it upside down on a clean piece of foil.

Gluing. Have the following at hand: a damp piece of sponge, which has been wrung out well; a damp cloth or honeycomb cloth (wrung out well); a small bowl of water.

Glue one piece at a time, starting with the largest or main piece. With your finger or a brush, spread the acrylic emulsion evenly onto the back of the glass where the print will go. Press the front of the cutout into the glue, and then, holding the damp cloth behind it, turn the glass to face you so that you can see that the print is in the right place. Any shiny spots you see are air bubbles that must be removed so that the glue will work properly. Use your fingers and the damp cloth to press these bubbles out, working from the center of the print to the edges. Work as quickly as possible, as acrylic emulsion dries very quickly. (Be careful not to press out *all* the emulsion.)

Remove excess glue from the edges of the cutouts with the damp sponge as you work and continue gluing until you are finished.

Check to be sure that all the pieces and their edges are firmly glued; add more glue with a toothpick or with a straight pin if it is necessary.

Your print will have a shiny look if you have removed too much glue. If this is the case, make a slit in the paper with a razor or a sharp knife and force more glue from the back to the front of the print.

Clean away any remaining excess glue with a cotton swab dipped in denatured alcohol, and wipe off the back of the glass with a damp cloth. (If you are working on plastic instead of glass, wipe away the denatured alcohol immediately, or it will make the plastic cloudy.) Remove china pencil markings with a damp paper towel, and rest the glass upside down on top of a jar to dry.

Note: Previously, decoupeurs glued under glass with either a white glue or a decoupage mucilage. Both glues are water soluble, but the mucilage is slower-drying than the white glue. If you use either of these glues, you must be sure to remove all excess glue between the print and the glass. Before the glue sets, press out any excess with your fingers, starting at the center and pressing toward the edges. Roll your finger against the glass, removing any air bubbles (which look like shiny spots) and pressing out as much glue as possible. The clear glass surface must be carefully and thoroughly cleaned with a damp sponge or a cotton-tipped swab to remove all glue. Dip your sponge in water to which you have added a few drops of white vinegar, wring it out well, and clean the glue off the glass. (Be careful—if there is too much water on the sponge, the print will come unglued.) Let the glue dry overnight and then check that all edges are glued down tight. If necessary, reglue loose edges, using a toothpick to force glue under the paper. With a fine brush dipped in sealer, coat all print edges, sealing them to the glass. Two thin coats of sealer over the entire glass surface and the back of the prints will protect the paper and provide a better bond for the painted background.

To guide you in placing your prints when you glue them under glass, trace outline of composition on front of glass and number with a china marker. With a pencil, number the cutouts on the *back* to correspond.

Sealing. When the glue is dry and clear on the top of the print, coat the entire back surface, print and all, with a thin, even coat of sealer or acrylic emulsion. *Pat* it on lightly with a soft brush or sponge and allow about 20 minutes for it to dry. (Don't brush it on or you'll see brushstrokes through the glass.) This coating of acrylic emulsion will seal the print to the glass so that paint cannot run or leak in front of the cutouts. It also provides a good bond for your background paint or paper.

Painting a background. Though there is a wide variety of backgrounds available to you when you decoupage under glass, it is best to start off with a simple background of acrylic paint. If applied carefully, this will give the effect of porcelain.

Do not brush paint or brushstrokes will show. *Pat* a thin, even coat of paint over the entire surface of the back of the glass, using a piece of soft sponge or a soft brush. Then rest the glass upside down on top of a jar or a can to dry; allow 12 hours drying time. Then apply a second coat of paint in the same way and allow another 12 hours drying time. (If you are using a transparent color, you may need a third coat of paint.)

If you use oil base paints rather than water base acrylics, allow at least 24 hours for each coat of paint to dry.

Clean off any paint from the edges or the top of the glass with a craft knife or a razor blade.

Finishing. To protect the paint from spotting or chipping, apply either two coats of varnish or one coat of acrylic emulsion and one coat of varnish after the paint has dried completely.

Optional. You may wish to glue a circle of felt to the bottom of glass objects such as plates and ashtrays. First, cut the felt to a slightly larger size than the bottom of your object. Then spread glue onto the bottom of your object and press the felt onto it evenly. Trim the edges. If your object curves up at the edges, make small V-shaped notches around the edge of the felt. Pull these together as you glue so that the felt fits smoothly. There are metallic braids and colored edgings that give a nice finished look when glued on top of felt around the edge of a plate.

Other backgrounds. You may wish to experiment with some other types of backgrounds after you have tried paint. The following is a list of background treatments that can be used under glass or plastic.

Gesso under glass produces a background that resembles porcelain. It can be tinted any color with a few drops of acrylic paint or with universal pigment.

Apply gesso by *patting* it on with a small sponge on the back of the glass. Let it dry for at least half an hour, and then brush on a second coat. If you are gessoing an object that will be washed frequently, such as a dinner plate, apply a minimum of eight coats of gesso, and seal *each* coat with plastic sealer. If your object will not be subject to very heavy use, two coats of gesso followed by two coats of varnish will suffice. The last coat of gesso should be dry

So your fingers won't stick to the paper cutouts, press out air bubbles (shiny spots) with a damp cloth.

Pat on background paint.

sanded with grade #400 (black) sandpaper until it is satin smooth.

If you want the bottom of your object to be colored, apply a coat of paint over your last coat of gesso, and then finish off with several coats of varnish.

Liquid metallic. This is a brush-on liquid that comes in several metallic shades—gold, silver, copper, and pewter, to name a few—and produces a rich, dramatic background.

Pat on the first coat, let it dry, and brush on a second coat. Then seal with plastic sealer, followed by a coat or two of varnish.

The solvent for liquid metallic is xylol.

Metallic wax. This finish comes in many colors, and can be used to provide several interesting effects. Apply with a sponge dampened with turpentine and *pat* on. To make swirls with metallic wax, dampen a large cotton ball with turpentine, dip the ball into the wax, and apply to the back of the glass with a light twisting motion. A soft brush used in the same way will produce a cloudlike effect. Try using a different color wax for the second coat—this will give the finish depth and a slightly textured quality. Let the wax dry for 12 hours, seal with plastic sealer, and then varnish.

The solvent for metallic wax is turpentine.

Liquid pearl or opaline. When patted on in thin coats, this finish has depth and is iridescent. It comes in several colors; when these are used in combination, the effect is something like opal or Tiffany glass. The intensity of the color will depend on the amount you use, the number of coats you apply, and your background color.

Apply thin coats, and allow at least half an hour drying time between coats. (Be sure to work in a well-ventilated room, as this is a lacquer base material, and the fumes are unpleasant.) Continue applying coats until the color is as intense as you want it. Allow the pearl to cure for several days before you apply paint behind it. When you do, use paint that is a shade darker than the pearl—red paint behind pink pearl, for example. Seal and then varnish.

The solvent for liquid pearl is lacquer thinner.

Rice paper. This paper can be used in combination with paint, liquid pearl, or liquid metallic to produce an effect similar to marble. Do not cut the paper, but *tear* it into small shapes no larger than 2 inches in diameter. Then glue the shapes onto the back of the glass, overlapping them slightly. When the glue is dry, apply color in any technique you wish (paint, liquid pearl, foil, or metallic wax). The paper will absorb the color, but the larger fibers of the paper will remain their original color. If you use very thin rice paper, you may wish to apply a second coat of torn shapes. Trim any protruding edges with a craft knife or a razor blade, seal, and varnish.

Tea paper. Silver or gold tea paper looks very elegant as a background under glass, especially in combination with Oriental prints. To antique gold tea paper, wipe it with a brown antiquing glaze. For silver tea paper, use a black antiquing glaze. Then seal.

For an interesting background, cut several layers of tea paper at a time into oval or circle shapes, and glue them onto the back of the glass so that they overlap in a random pattern. Let the glue dry, trim the edges of the paper, seal, and apply several coats of varnish.

Crackle. A product called "Crackle-It" produces a crackled effect that looks very good behind old prints. First, apply two coats of acrylic polymer emulsion to the back of your glass object. When dry, brush on a coat of "Crackle-It." The heavier the coat, the larger the cracks will be. Rub paint or an antiquing glaze into the cracks, and wipe away the excess. (You can apply "Crackle-It" before or after you glue on your print.) Finish off with a background coat of paint and several coats of varnish.

The solvent for "Crackle-It" is water.

(Right) Tea paper ovals make an elegant lining. (Below) The heart-shaped box was covered with pearl flakes (applied with glue) and then varnished for a sparkly, iridescent finish. The butterfly bowl has a crackle finish over two coats of acrylic polymer emulsion, with color rubbed into the cracks for an antique look. Rice paper was glued to the back of the plate on the left and then colored with metallic wax.

Hunting prints were used all over this antiqued ivory box (see page 58 for antiquing instructions). The iridescence and depth of the background in the glass lamp was achieved with two thin coats of blue liquid pearl, followed by blue paint (directions for applying liquid pearl are given on page 42). The plaque (one of a pair) was polished with oil and pumice for a very high gloss finish, and then polished with palm of hand for a special patina.

Glass Lamps

To progress from doing decoupage under a flat glass surface to working under a curved glass surface, such as a hurricane lamp, is both exciting and challenging. In addition to working on fine cutting and color harmony, you will have to pay particular attention to the composition of the many prints necessary to decorate a large, curved surface.

A straight glass hurricane is easiest to work on. Make sure the openings are large enough so that both your hands can fit inside the glass. If you are working on a curved hurricane lamp, use only small cutouts, as large ones will not lie flat on a curved surface.

Seal cutouts on the back and arrange them on the outside of the glass, attaching them temporarily with Plasti-tak. If you have a lazy Susan, use it so that you can turn the lamp on it and look at the composition from all sides.

After you have glued your prints down under the glass in the usual manner, paint the inside of the lamp by starting halfway up and working around the sides and out toward the bottom. Then turn the cylinder around, start from the center again, and work to the edges. When the background is finished, let the paint cure for at least a week.

When you assemble your lamp, do not screw the lock nut that holds the cap too tightly, or the glass will crack. Place a weight under the lamp base so that it will not tip over easily.

A simple silk or paper shade will set off your decoupage to its best advantage. You can, of course, trim or decorate a fabric or paper shade with decoupage that matches the lamp. Treat any print you plan to decoupage with two coats of acrylic polymer emulsion on the front. This will protect it from dust.

Use Plasti-tak to hold cutouts on exterior of glass while arranging, designing, and refining the final composition.

Then outline cutouts with china marker, showing exactly where to glue them under the glass.

Mirrors

Your decoupage can be applied to the mirror alone, or it can extend from the mirror out onto the frame.

Before you cut your print, color the *back* with black crayon or pencil (so that white edges will not be reflected in the mirror). Brush a coat of acrylic polymer emulsion over the print to protect it before cutting. (This is unnecessary if you plan to use glass over the mirror, as described below.) Then wash the mirror thoroughly with ammonia and water and dry with a lint-free cloth. (Hold the mirror at the edge so you do not smudge it with fingerprints.) Glue your cutouts to the mirror.

If your frame is deep enough, have a piece of ⅛ inch-thick glass cut to the size of your mirror. Make sure that the mirror and the protecting glass are completely dust-free before you insert them in the frame. Cover the back of the frame with brown paper to keep dust out.

If your frame is flat and simple, you may wish to cover it with fabric or wallpaper that matches the decor of your room. If you coat your fabric with acrylic emulsion it will not fray at the edges when you cut it out.

Mirrors can be fun. And with this one, anyone can be Venus! The print used here is a museum reproduction of a section of Botticelli's "Birth of Venus." Magazine covers featuring portraits could also be used—just cut out the face, and leave as much of the surrounding area as desired.

This hand-colored print was used as a cartouche, or frame, by cutting out the center section. The print was glued under glass, which was then gilded with Dutch metal for a formal look. A thin mirror was used behind the glass.

Various types of paper were cut out and arranged to create this "decollage" butterfly.

The high gloss black background and marbled flower prints lend an Oriental flavor to the large jewelry chest pictured here. Note the handsome brass hardware.

Advanced Techniques

Three-dimensional Decoupage

Three-dimensional decoupage (also called *papier tole, vue d'optique,* and *dimensionale*) is the technique of cutting apart several identical prints (a minimum of two, usually three), and then building them up in layers to create depth and perspective.

One print is used flat as the background, and succeeding layers (cut from the other prints) are glued to it with dabs of silicone adhesive. The amount of silicone used between each layer determines the elevation of each piece.

Silicone adhesive will remain flexible until it has set; it dries hard in approximately 24 hours. Excess silicone can be removed with a soft eraser. The prints used should be strong enough to mold and sculpt.

Work in 3-D is usually done on a wood surface or on fabric glued to wood, and is most effective in a shadow box, on a plaque, or in an inverted box top. (See page 16 for the basic techniques for preparing wood for decoupage.)

Cut apart several identical prints.

Materials
burnisher

silicone seal adhesive

tweezers

acrylic sealer

acrylic polymer emulsion

several identical prints

soft eraser

craft knife

glass or acetate plastic cut to size to cover the finished 3-D

Optional Supplies
oil base pencils

paints for touch-ups

clear crystal glaze

fine brush

Technique. Seal the front of the background print with two coats of acrylic sealer.

When dry, brush glue onto object and glue the print down, either directly onto the wood, or onto fabric and then to the wood.

Apply a heavy coat of acrylic polymer emulsion to the backs of your other prints. This will strengthen the paper and make it easier to contour.

Study your print before you do your cutting; there is a background

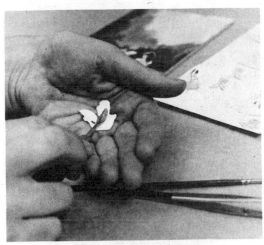
Contour cutouts with burnisher.

Build elevation with dabs of silicone.

The wedding invitation (applied to fabric and encircled by a floral cartouche), the delicate chinoiserie print, and the dancing ballerinas pictured here illustrate how effectively three-dimensional decoupage can be framed. The glass-topped box in the foreground, with its Daumier-print squirrels surrounded by a border of acorns, illustrates another way to display three-dimensional decoupage.

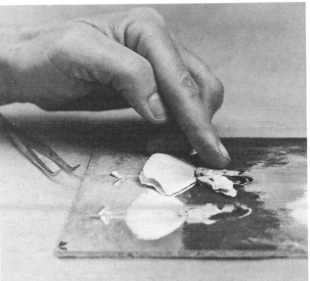

(farthest away), a middle ground, and a foreground (closest to the eye). From the matching prints, cut out the sections that are to be elevated.

Contour the cutouts by shaping them with your fingers and/or the flat end of a burnisher. Branches and leaves should be curved and sculpted and left freestanding, as in nature. Mushroom stems or columns can be wrapped around a pencil for a curved, rounded look. To round out a shape such as a flower, work from the center outward, holding the shape in the palm of your hand. Bend cutouts around a ruler to attain a sharp corner or an angle. Making tiny snips with your scissors or craft knife will help you to lift small sections of your print, such as petals. Cut many slivers to get a feathery effect.

Color the edges of your cutouts with oil base pencils, diluted paint, or felt-tipped markers. *Reseal.*

With dabs of the silicone adhesive, elevate the main pieces of the middle ground in proportion to their relationship to the whole. (Tweezers are helpful for positioning cutouts.)

Build up the elevation of the foreground pieces by repetition of prints and thicker applications of silicone.

Finishing touches (optional). Use a fine brush to apply several coats of clear crystal glaze to highlight those portions of your design that should look shiny (for instance, windowpanes).

Spray on a crystal clear glaze for an overall glossy porcelain finish.

Apply three coats of acrylic spray sealer for a low, even shine.

If you have used a shadow box frame or an inverted box top for your three-dimensional decoupage, cover it with glass or acetate. You can have glass cut to fit your specifications. Or you can purchase acetate plastic at a craft shop (it comes in standard sizes) and cut it with scissors to fit your frame or box.

(Above left) Use tweezers to position cutouts. (Above right) Use fingers to press in place, and to reposition cutout if it slides out of alignment with lower print.

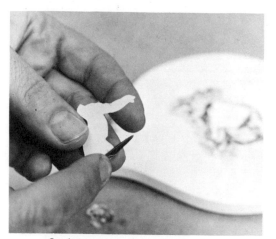

Sculpt cutouts from the back.

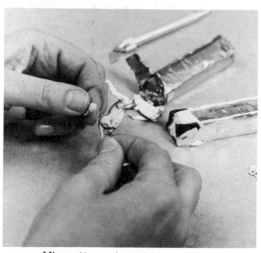

Mix putty and apply in ball to cutout.

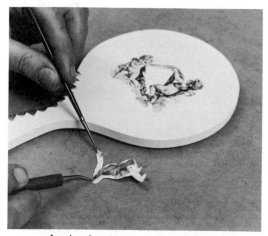

Apply glue to areas that will be flat.

Repoussé

Repoussé (pronounced re-poo-say) is a form of decoupage in which the cutting, preparation, and sculpting of prints creates a bas-relief effect. The object to be decoupaged is prepared as usual (see the section on Working With Wood: The Basic Techniques). Then a first print is glued down to the surface and one coat of finish is applied; this serves as the background for a second print, identical to the first, which is raised. The print to be repoussé (the second one) is cut apart; sections are then contoured and filled with a puttylike substance. Form is given to the print by actually sculpting it; it is then glued down to the identical section of the background print. The entire surface is then coated with varnish.

The prints used for this work should be on paper that is heavy enough to mold and sculpt.

Materials

burnisher
grade #0000 steel wool
acrylic sealer
acrylic polymer emulsion
paint
fine brush
white glue
two identical prints
varnish
hand-moldable epoxy
white wax
cloth or sponge

Preparation. Seal the front of the print to be repoussé with acrylic sealer, and then apply two coats of acrylic polymer emulsion to the back, allowing 15 to 20 minutes drying time between coats. (This will strengthen the paper so it can be contoured and sculpted.) Cut out the desired shapes.

Holding the cutouts face down in the palm of your hand, shape them from the back with your fingers and a burnisher. The light areas of your composition and the cutouts that will make up the foreground should be raised higher than dark areas and background sections.

Hand-moldable epoxy, which is also an adhesive, is the best "putty" material to use for filling the sculpted cutouts, though papier-mâché, ground up tissues bound with mucilage, or French clay mixed with glue can be used as well.

Technique. To mix hand-moldable epoxy (which comes in two sticks), cut an equal amount from each stick. Roll it together into a ball in your hands.

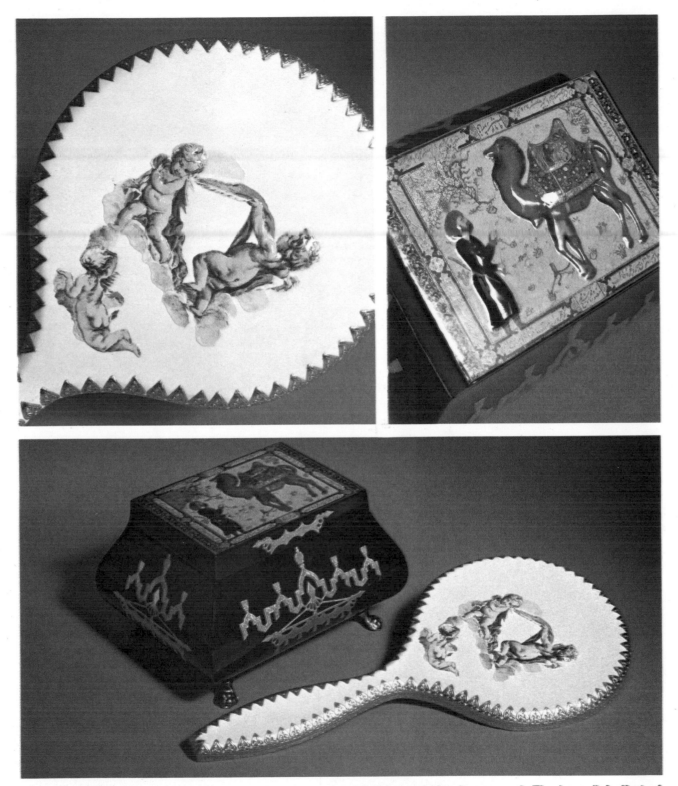

Figures, animals, birds, and fruit with rounded shapes are ideal for sculpting in repoussé. The bas-relief effect of rounded shapes raised in juxtaposition to flat prints creates an interesting focal point, as illustrated by the cupids on the mirror and the camel and driver on the box pictured here (details are shown above).

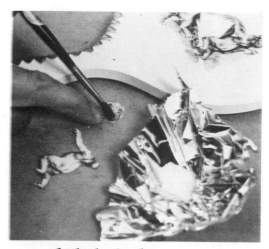

Apply glue to edges.

Press down glued edges with burnisher.

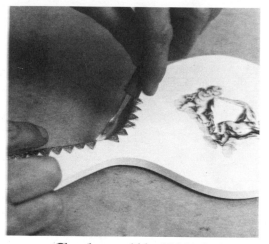

Glue down gold braid trim last.

After contouring the prints to be repousséd in the palm of your hand (as described above), mold the putty to your cutouts and shape as desired. For fullness and height use more putty; for a flatter look, use less.

Keep putty away from any edges that will be glued down flat. Coat these edges with glue, remove excess putty with the pointed end of your burnisher, and use the curved end of the burnisher to press the edges with glue down flat. (In shaping the edges of your prints, you may wish to leave some edges slightly raised, and some even higher, showing the putty; this is called a cookie-cutter edge.)

Clean the repousséd pieces with a damp cloth or a sponge and allow the putty to dry hard for at least an hour and a half.

After the putty is dry, touch up the raised edges to match the print with paint and a fine brush where the putty shows. If the prints need touching up, use your fingers and paint diluted with water rather than a brush. This will give the touched-up areas a transparent rather than a painted look.

Seal paint with acrylic sealer and apply varnish, going very lightly over the raised portions to prevent drips and buildup.

Wet sand all flat surfaces with grade #400 (black) wet-or-dry sandpaper. For a matte finish on repousséd portions, rub them very gently with #0000 steel wool wrapped around a cotton swab. Wash off, dry, and wax with white furniture wax.

Transferring Prints

Transferring a print is the process of lifting printing ink from paper to a clear plastic coating, using acrylic polymer emulsion as the transferring agent.

With this technique you can use pictures from newspapers, magazines, and calendars, and prints too intricate to cut out, for your decoupage projects.

Materials

paper or aluminum foil

masking tape

acrylic polymer emulsion

sponge applicator or nylon brush

rust-proof pan or dish for holding water

grade #400 (black) wet-or-dry sandpaper

brayer

varnish

Technique. Place the print to be transferred face up on clean paper or aluminum foil. Tape its edges down.

Using a nylon brush or a sponge applicator, apply six generous coats of acrylic emulsion over the print in alternating directions. Allow 15 to 20 minutes drying time between coats. (Place your brush or applicator in water between coats.)

Allow approximately 6 hours for the transfer to cure, and then remove tape from the print.

Soak the coated print in warm water to remove the paper from the back. Thin paper will peel away after about 3 hours of soaking; heavy paper will take longer (perhaps overnight).

When ready, place the wet print face down on a clean, hard, smooth surface. Keeping the transfer wet, rub gently with your fingers in a circular motion to remove the paper from the back.

Try not to stretch the transfer while you are doing this. When all the paper has come away, you will be left with a milky-looking film. This will eventually dry clear.

Your decorative transfer can now be applied to any number of different items, from wooden plaques and boxes to glass and metal objects.

Glue down your transfer with acrylic emulsion, and then roll over it gently with a brayer to fix it in place and to force out any air bubbles.

Brush on six to eight coats of acrylic emulsion in opposite directions, allowing 15 to 20 minutes drying time between coats.

Wet sand your project with grade #400 (black) sandpaper (see page 28 for directions on wet sanding).

Apply three or four coats of varnish for protection.

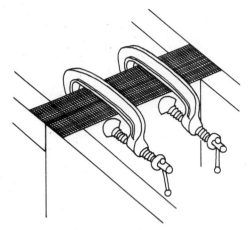

Use C-clamps to hold lid in place while glued fabric hinge sets.

Fabric Hinges

Fabric hinges may be used on some boxes in place of metal hinges. They are almost invisible, and should only be used on small boxes with lightweight lids.

Materials

acrylic polymer emulsion

nylon georgette

two C-clamps or clothespins

nylon brush or sponge

dish of water

Technique. After sanding your box in the usual manner, attach the top to the bottom in the open position with two small C-clamps. Match the edges as evenly as possible.

Cut a strip of nylon georgette to fit the width and the length of the edges to be hinged.

Apply a coat of acrylic emulsion to the edges to be hinged.

Place the strip of fabric onto the wet emulsion. Allow 30 minutes drying time, and then apply four more coats; let the emulsion dry thoroughly between coats.

Remove the C-clamps and trim away excess fabric.

Paint lightly over the fabric hinge when you paint the inside of your box. When you apply finish to the box, go lightly over the hinge, or the buildup of finish will keep the box from closing properly.

Gilding

Applying gold leaf to wood or glass as a background for decoupage is a technique that requires some skill, but with care and practice, it affords beautiful results.

Composition leaf, called Dutch metal, is much less expensive than real 24-karat gold leaf. It is available in books of 25 sheets. Each 5½ × 5½-inch sheet is separated by a page of tissue (or rouge) paper. Aluminum leaf, which looks like silver but will not tarnish, is especially effective under glass, as it provides a mirrorlike background.

Work in as dust-free and draft-free an area as possible when using these delicate leaves.

Materials

book of gold, silver (aluminum), or marbled leaf

sizing (fast-drying adhesive)

talcum powder

cotton balls

tweezers

plastic sealer

varnish

Preparation. Your surface should be clean, dry, and smooth.

If your object is made of wood, sand it smooth, seal it, and then apply a coat of paint as a base. Traditionally, dark red paint is used as a background for gold leaf, and black paint is used for silver; these undercoatings enhance the gold and silver with a tinted glow.

If the surface to be gilded is very grainy or porous, apply at least two coats of gesso to it, and then sand it until it is very smooth. Follow the sanding with a polishing, using grade #0000 steel wool; then seal and apply a base coat of paint.

If you are gilding under glass, clean the glass with ammonia, rinse well, and dry it thoroughly before proceeding.

Technique. Sizing, or gold-leaf adhesive, binds the leaf to the surface to be gilded. A fast-drying size will become tacky in just a few minutes. Apply a thin coating of adhesive and wait until it is tacky. Test it with your knuckle; it is ready if you hear a slight "clicking" sound and your knuckle comes away from the surface with a soft pull.

Cut the thread from the book and cut the leaves at the edge so you can handle one sheet at a time (or cut sheets in quarters). Use a little talcum powder on your fingers to keep them from getting sticky, and use tweezers or a pointed knife to help lift a piece of leaf. Handle the leaf as delicately as possible; it will crumble if handled roughly.

Using the tissue papers to hold the leaf top and bottom, slide the bottom piece of tissue down about an inch, and lay that inch of leaf on the sizing. Slide the bottom tissue away slowly as you lay the leaf down, until the entire piece has been applied. Do this carefully, so that the leaf lies flat. Press down gently from center out with the top tissue so that the leaf adheres to the sizing on the surface of your object, and then remove the tissue.

Apply the leaves so that they overlap about ¼ inch. Large cracks or tears can be patched with scraps so that they don't show; wrinkles will disappear with burnishing (see below). Small cracks in the leaf which allow the base paint to show through have an attractive antique look; often the gold leaf is broken in this way on purpose.

Let the sizing dry for several hours before you start to burnish. Then polish the leaf with a ball of soft cotton or a very soft, dry brush. Gently rub away wrinkles and any excess overlapping leaf, and smooth seams.

Apply a coat of plastic sealer to prevent the leaf from tarnishing. (For an antique finish, let the sealer dry, apply antique finish following the directions on page 58, apply another coat of sealer, and then varnish.)

After applying your decoupage, build up your varnish finish.

Antiquing

The art of antiquing is a simple one. It requires little practice to achieve a mellow, aged look on a brand-new surface. A fine example is illustrated on page 60.

Antiquing glazes are readily available at most hardware and paint stores in various shades of black, brown, blue, green, rust, and honey. (The most popular shade seems to be raw umber—a deep, warm brown.) Traditionally, glazes are oil based, soluble in turpentine, and slow-drying. Today, however, there are water base glazes available that dry very quickly, have no odor, and can be cleaned up with water.

You can make your own antiquing glaze by mixing together three parts turpentine, three parts varnish, and one part oil paint. To make a water base glaze, mix water with a water base paint. Metallic waxes and liquid gold paint can be thinned and used as glazes for a rich effect.

Materials

varnish

plastic gloves

antiquing glaze

soft cloth or brush

clean cloth, paper towels, or cheesecloth

Technique. Since it is easier to control antiquing over varnish than it is over paint, varnish your object after you have painted and decoupaged it, and then apply your glaze. Wear a pair of plastic gloves to protect your hands, and apply your glaze with a cloth or a brush. Cover the entire surface of your object.

Remove excess glaze with paper towel.

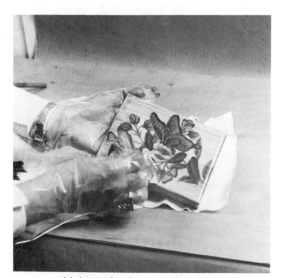
Lighten further as desired, especially over the print surface.

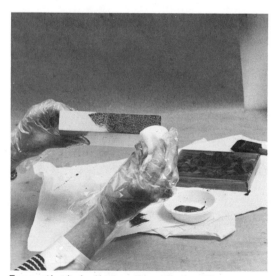
For a stippled effect, pat on glaze with a sponge.

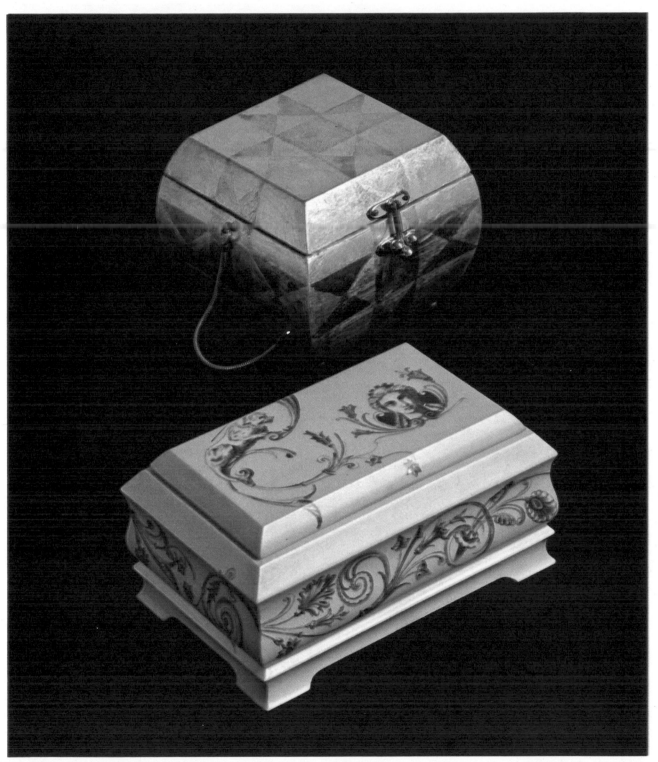

The purse illustrated here is an elegant example of the results that can be achieved when gold and silver leaf are applied to wood. The geometric design is accented by a gold "snake" chain. The attractive yellow box is decorated with hand-colored prints in the grisaille palette, illuminated with touches of gold leaf. The interior of this box is black, and features a piece of the print autographed in gold.

Antiquing glaze mellowed the ivory background for these old hunting prints.

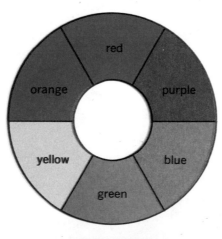

COLOR WHEEL

The three primary colors are red, yellow, and blue. Secondary colors are made from the primary colors: red and yellow make orange, blue and yellow make green, and red and blue make purple.

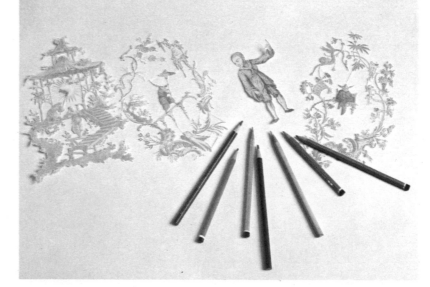

Use the same palette to hand color all the prints for one project. For instance, the single gray figure here was not used with the three chinoiserie prints, which were cut apart and rearranged to decorate a turquoise knife box.

In about a minute, start wiping off the glaze with long, smooth strokes, using a clean cloth or a crumpled paper towel. Wipe off in one direction, and do it carefully, as this will determine how the antiquing glaze looks. It is the wiping away that achieves the desired effect, so you will want to practice a bit. For instance, try adding more glaze at the corners, or other areas where dirt would have settled on an old box, and leave central areas lighter. Add a little more glaze in carved and recessed areas and at the edges. Perhaps you'll want to remove more glaze to let the print show better. Lighten areas you have made too dark with a cloth dipped in solvent. If you're not satisfied, remove it all and start again.

Crumpled paper towels or crumpled, thin plastic can be pressed down on the glaze while it is still wet and then picked up carefully to make random markings. Experiment for different effects.

Near disasters can often be rescued by antiquing. Applying glaze heavily to damaged areas, and more lightly to surrounding areas, will often improve the object's appearance. Try patting the glaze on with an even-grained synthetic sponge, working from the damaged area to lighter areas as the color goes out of the sponge. Try for an even stippled effect.

Allow the glaze to dry thoroughly. (Oil base glazes take 24 hours to dry; water base glazes take about 30 minutes.) Then apply a coat of clear finish to protect your glaze.

Note: Glazes can be used on hinges and hardware, if they look too shiny, and on embossed gold paper and gold leaf to soften their brightness if desired.

To antique a print only, wipe it with cold tea or coffee; this will stain the paper an attractive, light brown color.

Hand Coloring

Traditional eighteenth-century decoupage was done with black and white prints that were colored in by hand. Today, "heirloom" pieces are hand colored for richness, depth, and beauty.

The art of coloring requires a knowledge of color basics and color harmony, and some mastery of the techniques of coloring and shading with oil base pencils. Practice, patience, and concentration will help you in mastering your coloring technique. Study the simple color wheel on page 60 and then experiment with making your own colors. Combine primary colors to make secondary colors. Then try combining a primary color with a secondary color that is next to it on the color wheel. (For instance, use red over orange to get a red-orange.) Experimenting on your own this way will help you learn about color relationships and harmonies.

Note: Because of their different qualities, it isn't advisable to combine hand-colored and pre-colored prints in the same project. Hand-colored decoupage looks like hand-painted art, and the reproduction is easily distinguished from the original.

Materials

black and white prints on matte paper

oil base pencils (Derwent, Prismacolor, or Colorama)

soft eraser

hand pencil sharpener (for a fine point)

plastic sealer

Technique. Place a smooth cardboard surface under your print, support your arm on the working surface, and hold your pencil at an angle. Press evenly, but not hard.

Keeping your pencil on the paper, practice blending smooth, even strokes together. All printed lines should be colored.

Blend from dark to light, starting off with dark printed lines and blending into lighter areas. Your coloring should not be opaque; let the lines of the print show through. Stroke your pencil in the direction of the printed lines, following the shapes of the areas you are coloring. Try to blend your strokes together lightly and evenly so that individual strokes don't show.

Leave highlights uncolored, and then go over them with white pencil. (If you forget to leave highlights, erase your color and then use white pencil.)

Use your eraser to lighten printed lines that are too dark, or to lighten areas that you have colored in too heavily.

Note: Intensity of color is achieved by repeated application of color, not pressure. The old masters achieved depth in their painting by applying one transparent glaze over another, even in the darkest areas. Keep your work transparent, not opaque.

Some suggestions. Study the color wheel; it will help you choose your palette. Select a simple one at the outset. For example, three shades of one color—a dark, a medium, and a light shade—will do at first. Shade from dark to medium to light, and then blend the shades together by going over the entire area with the lightest pencil.

Try outlining some of the more interesting lines and curves in the print with the darkest shade (using a very sharp, pointed pencil). This gives depth to the coloring and sharpens the design.

Balance your colors. Let two or three colors predominate, rather than using an equal amount of every color.

To achieve perspective, make your colors brighter and more distinct as they come to the foreground. Objects in the background should be paler and grayer. Fill in color working from the background to the foreground, making details more distinct and colors brighter as you come forward.

Hand-colored prints that will be covered with varnish must be colored much brighter than those that will be placed under glass. If you plan to use varnish, test your colors by placing the print you have colored under a clear piece of glass that has been coated with twenty coats of varnish. If your colors do not look bright enough, apply more.

Note: Seal all the prints you have colored before cutting them out.

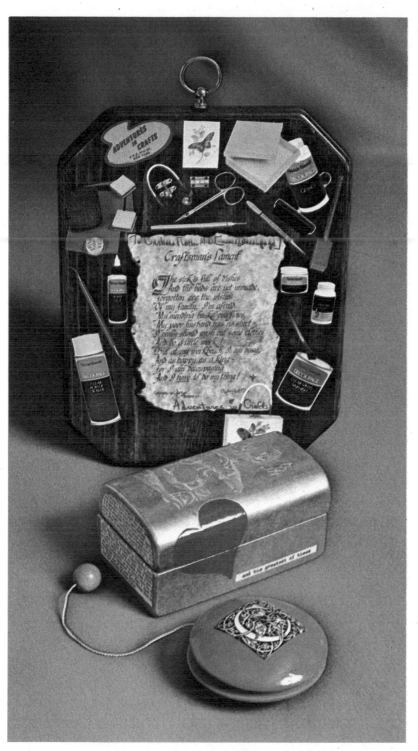

The stained wooden plaque above features the "Craftsman's Lament," and pictures of the tools and materials used to make a student's first project. The Valentine Box sports a red felt heart and "LOVE" letters cut from a plastic shopping bag. The Executive Yo-Yo was painted and then monogrammed with initials from an old book.

This charming nursery light was made from a raw wood cylinder lamp. Matching yellow velvet ribbon was glued to the lampshade. The wooden switchplate was painted and decoupaged to be used with the lamp.

Bibliography

Cennini, Cennino, *The Craftsman's Handbook.* Reprinted by Dover Publications, Inc., New York, N.Y., 1933.

Grotz, George, *The Furniture Doctor.* Doubleday & Co., Inc., Garden City, N.Y., 1962.

Harrower, Dorothy, *Decoupage—A Limitless World in Decoration.* Bonanza Books, New York, N.Y., 1968.

Honour, Hugh, *Chinoiserie.* Harper & Row Publishers, New York, N.Y., 1973.

Ladies' Amusement Book or The Whole Art of Japanning Made Easy. Reprinted by The Ceramic Book Co., St. John's and Chepstow Rd., Newport, Monmouthshire, Wales, 1959.

Manning, Hiram, *Manning on Decoupage.* Hearthside Press, Inc., Great Neck, N.Y., 1969.

Mitchell, Marie, *The Art of Decoupage.* Marie Mitchell's Decoupage Center, Detroit, Mich., 1966.

———— *Advanced Decoupage.* Marie Mitchell's Decoupage Center, 1971.

Newman, Thelma, *Contemporary Decoupage.* Crown Publishers, Inc., New York, N.Y., 1972.

Nimocks, Patricia, *Decoupage.* Charles Scribner's Sons, New York, N.Y., 1968.

O'Neil, Isabel, *Art of the Painted Finish for Furniture and Decoration: A House and Garden Book.* William Morrow & Co., Inc., New York, N.Y., 1971.

Sommer, Elyse, *Decoupage Old and New.* Watson Guptill Publications, Inc., New York, N.Y., 1971.

Wing, Frances, *Complete Book of Decoupage.* Coward, McCann & Geoghegan, Inc., New York, N.Y., 1965.

Suppliers

Most of the materials mentioned in this book are available at craft, department, and hardware stores. Unless otherwise noted, the following suppliers sell both retail and mail order.

Brandon's Memorabilia
1 West 30th St.
New York, N.Y.
(for gold braid and prints)

Singerie
914 S. Robertson Blvd.
Los Angeles, Calif. 90035

Carson & Ellis
1153 Warwick Ave.
Warwick, R.I. 02888
(for tinware)

Dick Blick
P.O. Box 1267
Galesburg, Ill. 61401

Sax Arts and Crafts
P.O. Box 2002
Milwaukee, Wis. 53201

Morris Manufacturing Co.
3837 Dividend St.
P.O. Box 1527
Garland, Texas 75042
(mail order only)

Hazel Pearson Handicrafts
4128 Temple City Blvd.
Rosemead, Calif. 91770

Harrower House of Decoupage
37 Carpenter St.
Box 502
Milford, N.J. 08848

Adventures in Crafts
218 East 81st St.
New York, N.Y. 10028

Marie Mitchell's
   Decoupage Center
16111 Mack Ave.
Detroit, Mich. 48224

Manning Studio of Decoupage
41 Upton St.
Boston, Mass. 02118

Lee Wards
1200 St. Charles St.
Elgin, Ill. 60120
(mail order address)

ABCDEF